# SIT DOWN | SIT UP

*By*

*Tobi Akinyemi*

Copyright © 2019 by Tobi Akinyemi

All rights reserved. No part of this book may be reproduced or used in any manner without written permission of the copyright owner except for the use of quotations in a book review.

For more information, address: info@thehappyman.xyz

First paperback edition April 2019

*Book design by* **The Design Bloc**

ISBN 978-0-244-17252-7

www.thehappyman.xyz

*A man [who is held] in honour, yet who lacks [spiritual] understanding and a teachable heart, is like the beasts that perish.*
*{Psalms 49:20 Amp}*

*This book is dedicated to every single person that invested in me, never gave up on me or contributed to my growth in some way...*
*Thank you!*

# Contents

Preface 1

Welcome to life     7

Life 0.1     13

More memories – I remember     19

"Posted on the block like a…"     25

Off to university…     33

Life of the party     41

**Extract from 'Misconceptions' by Debrae 51**

I love girls, girls, girls, girls…. 53

White shirt gang     59

Africa o'clock!     65

Good credit or Image? 73

**'Dark' – Debo     79**

Clouds     81

**'Warrior' – Debrae     85**

The conversation!     87

TLC way!     95

Life 1.0     99

No magic, no tricks?     109

*The struggles*    115

*Common mistakes?*    121

*Bolts, nuts & spanner*    125

*The gains*    135

*Let's measure: Any growth yet?*    141

*The secret ammunition!*    149

**Friends for sale –Ehae Longe (Inktippeddreams)**    165

*Managing people in my grey years*    167

*You are not alone - #MeToo!*    181

*Feeling the pressure yet?*    191

**Extract from 'I am More' by Tolu Fabiyi**    199

*The question I get asked all the time*    201

*Dear entrepreneurs/creatives*    211

*Who gon' stop us now?*    217

**Extract from 'The Race' by Tolu Fabiyi**    221

*Epilogue*    223

**Transformation – Princess Ashilokun**    229

*Acknowledgements*    231

# Preface

*If anyone had ever told me, 'Tobi, one day you will write a book', I would probably have replied saying, 'you are a high-flying bluffer'.*

I have always been an interesting character. Sometimes I even fascinate myself. Perhaps that's why some friends say that when they think of me, the first thing that comes to mind is, 'what a character'. I was excluded from primary school, kicked out of sixth form, and was on my last warning in University. The security panel had said to me on my third visit to them, 'if you ever come into this interrogation room again, you are out of this university'

Becoming an author wasn't something I had ever thought of. It all started when my friend Tolu asked me to be part of the panel at her book launch. It was an honour and a surprise because I wasn't sure why she asked me to be a panellist, of all the people she could have chosen. While I sat there on the panel, I heard a soft voice say, 'it is time to scribe'. I left it. On my way home, I was dropping off a friend and we were talking about vulnerability. She shared how she was vulnerable with an ex-boyfriend and he ended up using it against her. It didn't sound like a nice experience, she sounded like she had been scarred from that relationship. I shared some experiences and talked about how I was trying to rewrite my life story. She then said, 'I think you should write a book. It would be a lot of work but think about it'. This was the second time in the day, but I just ignored it and I later said to her that I would start by blogging, which she volunteered to help proof- read and edit if necessary.

The final straw was on a Friday evening. Earlier in the day, I got the nudge to start putting titles of chapters together for a potential book. I hadn't prayed about writing and was just putting a framework together. I went for a prayer meeting and my main prayer point was for God to speak to me about the book. I wanted him to give me a sign that I should write it. A while into the prayers, Uche, who was leading the prayers that day, randomly said, 'I see books in this room. I see some of you writing books. In fact, it is like God has given you everything you need for it already and you are just doubting yourself'. This was it! It felt spooky but that was the moment it all clicked.

I have experienced life in different shades. I have slept in 5-star hotels for nights and I have also slept on the farm in the middle of nowhere just counting down till sunrise. I have flown first and business class and have also ridden on a rented bicycle in Oyo State, Nigeria. I have dined with celebrities and partied with footballers, but have also eaten with the people of Bakatari (a remote village just outside Ibadan, Oyo state). I have been chauffeur-driven in a Rolls Royce but have also driven a truck full of watermelons and cucumbers from Ibadan to Lagos at late hours on the notorious Lagos-Ibadan expressway.

I have experienced quite a lot of things at an earlier stage than most of my peers, so my outlook on life has always been different. At various stages in my life, I was motivated differently compared to my peers. When I would have conversations with people, I would usually not be surprised or fascinated by what they were sharing, and it is because I had experienced, seen or heard those things before. Sometimes, it makes me feel like I grew up too fast.

Having entertainment as my background was one of the best things to happen to me. It taught me not to believe everything I see. It taught me to value people but not their opinion. It taught me that if you can freeze a moment into a picture, what happened before and after that picture (the reality) doesn't matter. 'Fake it till you make it' was the reality. During this phase of what people would have seen as me 'living my best life', I had an awakening and the game changed.

There's an awakening we will all experience at some point in our lives, some earlier than others. I personally believe that you really start living the day your awakening happens and you respond to it. The awakening is a liberating moment, the day all baggage starts to fall off and weights are lifted off your shoulder.

Before this point, I had been pursuing wealth, power and maybe fame, but I later realised that all these things wouldn't satisfy me. I had a void that needed to be filled. Right now, with less of all these things, I am extremely content, and it is an 'out of this world' feeling, it is liberating and peaceful. With the new lifestyle came a lot of challenges, some of which I still struggle with.

The journey is personal to everyone, because our experiences are different and they shape who we become. You might have been born looking like your parents but you will die looking like your decisions, so as much as you experience an awakening, it is your personal decision to be responsive to it. Nobody can help you do that. It would be tough and like me, you might try a '6 months taster' to see if it is really worth it. I can tell you now for free - *it is*.

This book is in three parts: The first part is about my background and delves into the sheer extent of my 'naughtiness'; the second part is about my awakening and how I managed and struggled with it initially; and the third part is about how I am managing it now despite the distractions, as well as what I have learned.

*Technical note: In parts of this book, I have changed people's names. This is especially where it's a sensitive story. An example, I spoke about a family friend that died. His death was a big blow, and in the context of how I spoke about him, I couldn't mention his name.*

# Welcome to life

On a hot summer day, I was born at Our Lady's Catholic hospital, in a small town called Iseyin, in Oyo State, Nigeria. Apparently, my birth had come with many complications. My mum was in Lagos and was getting ready to head out to London when she received a phone call from her cousin, Aunty Nike. Aunty Nike had also been her chief bridesmaid, so they are really close. Aunty Nike called to say that a missionary had just come into her salon and said to her, 'you have someone quite close to you who is pregnant and about to leave the country for London in a few days. Call her right away and tell her that she must not go, or she will lose that child.' It is important to remember that in those days, mobile phones were hard to come by and she had only just got a phone installed in her salon. It was fortunate that we also had one.

The crazy thing is that Aunty Nike knew my mum was pregnant, but she did not know that my mum was planning a trip. The last time they had spoken, my mum told her she was going to Lagos but didn't specify when. After my Aunty received the message from the missionary, she called two of her friends she knew were pregnant to find out if either of them was the person spoken about, but neither of them were planning to leave the country anytime soon, so she left it at that but with the message still lingering on her mind. The day after, she felt a prompt to call my mum for a catch-up and to tell her about the random message from the missionary. When she rang my parents' house, my cousin picked up the phone and told her that my mum had already gone to Lagos. At that point, she suspected that the message could be for my mum.

In an effort to clarify if the woman spoken about was my mum, she asked to speak to my dad. He confirmed that my mum was in Lagos and would be traveling in three days but they didn't talk about where she was going. Then, she called the house of my Aunty who my mum was staying with in Lagos, so that she could speak to my mum and tell her what the missionary said. She found out that my mum would be travelling to London. So, the missionary was spot-on: My mum was the person he was referring to. It was my mum who was about to travel to London and I was the baby she was carrying. Thankfully, my mum listened and rescheduled her trip to London until after the birth. Who knows what would have happened.

My mum didn't have a complicated delivery but according to her, another major incident happened when I was 6-month-old. I became really ill and the paediatricians had said that the chance of survival was slim (it was a scary situation because my family was already losing hope). I was in the hospital for a very long time. However, by the amazing grace of God, with the help of some intercessors who were fasting and praying, and through the work of the paediatricians, I was able to recover. I have a huge scar from this on my left hip joint that is still very visible today. It is quite long and lined along my pelvis and apparently, it is where the doctors cut me open at the hospital because they could not find veins. So much history before I could even walk!

I was a very mischievous child. Every time I meet someone who knew me as a child, they always have a story to tell and it is usually E-P-I-C. There is one story in particular that I still find to be really funny. I was about three years old and was at home with just my paternal grandmother. She had come around to look after my sister Tomi and I, as my parents were not around and our domestic staff had taken some time off over the Christmas break. Usually we had my maternal great grandmother around, but she was with my cousins for

Christmas that year, so my paternal grandmother decided to come and help out for a while. She wasn't used to me, so she would let me have my way even though my mum had warned her to always keep an eye on me and make sure I wasn't out of sight. On this particular day, my sister had started crying, so I thought this meant that she was hungry and I went to open a new can of baby formula (my mum always got Cerelac in the largest can). I emptied all of the baby formula in the bathtub and opened the tap. My grandmother heard the tap running and at about the same time, realized I had been gone for a while. She was scared and hoped that I hadn't drowned or that something crazy hadn't happened to me, because she kept calling for me and I wasn't replying. I couldn't hear her because the tap was running and I was too busy prepping the formula for my sister! She finally got to the bathroom and saw me sitting in the bath with the tap running and an empty can of Cerelac on the floor. 'Tobi!' She shouted. 'What are you doing?!' 'Granny, I am making food for Tomi because she was crying!' She froze for some seconds because she didn't know how to respond – why child why?!

As I mentioned earlier, my maternal great grandmother (Mama) usually lived with us. It was easy to offend and run to her because Mama was my saviour. This was why I always felt Mama's absence, because anytime I got into trouble while Mama was away on a trip, I got disciplined. I remember a time that I upset my mum. She was furious and tried to grab me, but I was too quick and managed to escape her reach and run to Mama. Usually, when I would run to Mama, my mum would not come after me. However, this day was different. Believe me when I say that my typically forgiving mum came after me to where Mama sat, tried to hit me but missed and hit Mama in the face instead. Mama, an octogenarian at the time, was dazed. Her eyes eventually became swollen, she was unable to walk for a couple of days and it became so bad that Mama had to receive medical treatments at home. What a child I was.

# Life 0.1

When I became a little older, I aspired to be either a pilot or an engineer of some sort because those were the only professions I knew – Thanks Dad! However, I found being a pilot more appealing than being an engineer because I wanted to 'drive' my personal Boeing 747. I would have parking space for it in my hangar outside my well-landscaped 20-bed mansion with a lot of space for a football pitch, a basketball court and a swimming pool. This was all I wanted when I grew up. #Goals

My dad worked for a telecommunications company as a Head Engineer, which might explain why he really wanted me to be an engineer of some sort, or a pilot at the very least. He would buy me toy planes, hoping that they would fascinate me and that I would maybe fall in love with them, but I destroyed them most of the time. Due to the nature of his job, he was moved around quite a lot and was always traveling. When it was time for me to start nursery school, for the sake of stability and a better education, my parents moved me to Lagos to live with my dad's older sister. I attended Doland International School before my dad was moved again and my parents decided to settle in Ibadan, in Oyo state. I have more memories of Ibadan than of any of the other cities or towns I lived in. I went to Lifeforte International School, where I was one of the most notorious kids in my school year, if not the most notorious.

I was so naughty that my mum said she felt it was a dream (more like a nightmare) at times. Even from my time in nursery at Doland, my Aunty (who I lived with) was invited to come in for meetings. I moved to Lifeforte at prep grade (bridge between nursery and primary) and the school invitations didn't stop. The first fixed period exclusion I can really recollect was in 3rd grade and I was seven years old then. Another memorable incident happened in 3rd grade with my class teacher, Mr. Alabi. Mr. Alabi was a calm teacher, but I must have provoked him quite a bit that day. I honestly cannot remember the details, but I remember the aftermath vividly.

At school, the teachers tried as much as possible not to use the cane but sometimes it had to be done, especially with frustrating kids such as myself. Mr. Alabi caned me so badly that my hands were swollen and ached for days. When I got home and my mum saw them, she was so upset and insisted that she would come with me to school the next day. This was unexpected of my mum knowing how stubborn and troublesome I was, she had usually encouraged the teachers to beat me. The next day, she came and gave them an earful. The Indian Head Teacher Ms. Silva had to apologise, and so did Mr. Alabi. He was initially unrepentant until my mum threatened to take the matter to the owners/proprietress of the school and also bring in my dad. My dad is the calmest of people- He is cheeky, funny, and quite low-profile most times. He can be quiet, but when he gets angry- holy lord! My sisters and I never received a beating from him growing up, even with my stubbornness and all the trouble I got into. However, there was a day that he decided to 'teach' my sister 'a lesson'. That day, my mum joined in my sister's crying even though she wasn't the one that got the beating. Mr Alabi didn't know my dad but Ms. Silva had seen him get angry before, we lived quite close to eachother. Perhaps my father's reputation preceded him, so they had to be repentant.

I was away from school for about two days and when I came back, Mr. Alabi had a conversation with me – a father/son type of conversation. The words he spoke have remained with me until today. He also taught me a life lesson that day. It was time for another class prefect to be elected, it was a weekly rotation and the position needed to be contested. To my surprise, he nominated me. I had never thought of contesting because it came with what I believed to be too much responsibility and commitment. The people who became class prefects were usually the 'nerds' – the ones who always did their homework, were 'well-behaved' and were the teachers' favourites. I had to contest for it against a guy that was just a pure nerd and didn't really have any friends. I thought I would have it in the bag. I was more excited by the opportunity to boss my classmates around, I also had some classmates that always wrote my name down as a noisemaker when the class teacher wasn't in, so this was an opportunity to retaliate and get them in trouble because I would be the most powerful 3rd grader– hello power! Fortunately for those classmates, the opposition won and not just a close win, but an actual demolition job– he had 14 votes and I had just one (from my boy Bolu, a real friend from early on.) Even my close family friends didn't vote for me! I had it all wrong, clearly being popular did not mean that I would be the people's choice. The people's choice was usually a responsible leader. At that young age, people in my year had seen that I was popular for all the wrong reasons and definitely was not responsible enough to lead or represent them.

I will always remember that day. I learnt an important life lesson. In Mr. Alabi's words, 'you can be known, but not relevant. My friend, be relevant!' As young as I was then, it stuck with me and from that day on, I decided that I would be relevant. However, I guess the next question is, be relevant for what?

# More memories – I remember

I remember being woken up on Sunday mornings to get ready for Church by our domestic staff. When we would get to church, the destination would be the children's church, but some of my family friends (Jayeade, Damola, Jide), myself and a few others would sneak out and walk around the church instead because we didn't want to read/watch bible stories. It was a really massive church- Winners Chapel. Church security and the traffic control guys would chase us on numerous occasions. I remember my mum asking me once, 'I hope you aren't one of the kids that roam around during service?' I am sure you can guess my answer- NO! Another thing we used to do was take out the offering our parents gave us from the envelopes and buy sweets with the money instead, we didn't know any better!

I remember frustrating my Ghanaian home tutor to the point that he said he wasn't going to teach us anymore. He came to the house to tutor Tomi and I every day after school. Suddenly, he just stopped showing up and when my mum called him to ask what was happening, he told her how I was so different from my sister, so stubborn and naughty. He said that his youngest child was in university and none of his kids had ever stressed him so much, so he was done with tutoring us – well me especially.

I remember being chased by the police in our estate in New Bodija. In the monthly estate meeting, they had agreed that over the Christmas holiday, there should be no fireworks due to the security issues, as a lot of armed robberies were happening. As kids, we didn't listen to the warning delivered by our parents, we went ahead and put money together, buying out all the fireworks from the local estate supermarket – why were they even selling them? On New Year's Eve, we all came out and started with the fireworks. These three non-uniform police officers walked into the gates of our estate. I still do not understand how I managed to escape them and run into our house. Some of the other kids got arrested and ended up staying at the police station into the New Year! The estate security men tried to stop them from taking anyone, but they couldn't stop them as they were police officers.

I remember going into my mum's bag to steal money on a few occasions. I honestly do not remember what I used the money for. Also, I remember fighting Funmi, one of the domestic staff on numerous occasions because she would catch me 'taking' meat from the cooking pot and she would threaten me with this default statement, 'I am going to report you to mummy'. I guess that children's song was about me – *who stole the meat from the cooking pot?*

After my junior secondary school education in Crown Heights College, my parents had considered sending Tomi and I over to London, but changed their minds because they felt that one of them had to be there to live with us, especially me. Instead, they decided to send me to a strict school in Nigeria. An old friend of theirs told them about a relatively new school in Ibadan started by a Baptist Church with students who were winning national awards. My dad, who was Baptist-born and grew up in a Baptist household, was excited about this and this is how I ended up in Oritamefa Baptist Model School (OBMS). The level of discipline at OBMS was higher than what I got in my old school and at home put together. You had to wear a certain colour of socks and shoes, and there were hairstyles dictated for the girls weekly. In my entire educational life, that was the first time I had not looked forward to going to school because I would always get into trouble and receive punishment for one reason or the other. OBMS was also my first experience of getting punished because I got punished, if that makes sense. Mr A punishes you for doing something wrong then Mr B sees you being punished and says, 'when you are done, I am going to punish you for getting punished'.

That chapter ended and finally it was time to move to England. I remember sleeping on MSN Messenger chatting to females and planning link-ups. 'Free yard' (where no one is at home) was a constant for me because my parents were back and forth between Nigeria and the UK, so I got to do whatever I wanted most times. When either of my parents were around, I would sneak out at silly hours of the night to go to my link's house– especially the ones whose parents worked night shifts. Obviously, before their parents got back in the morning, I would have gone home and snuck back in. I once had to jump out of the window to escape after we had over-slept.

I remember coming home with my right ear pierced. I initially started wearing magnetic earrings. I would wear them and then take them off just before I went home. My friends then found out that I wore magnets and would tease me about it. So I decided to actually pierce my ear after all, I was about that life – I could do whatever I liked. I went to the piercing shop and after they were through, they told me not to remove the stud for six weeks and to turn and clean it daily, giving me some liquid to clean it with. I thought I would be able to take it out and put it back in like I did with the magnets, I didn't know it came with those extra measures. My mum wasn't around anyway she was in Nigeria and wasn't going to be back for a few weeks. I decided that I would worry about hiding it from her when the time came.

I got a shocker when I got home and heard her voice. I could hear her voice and was trying to convince myself that it wasn't her. She was back! How could she be back? I walked into the living room and she was there. She noticed the piercing immediately, asking and giving an order in the same sentence:

'Tobi what is that? Remove it before I open my eyes!'

'I can't remove it, I have to wait for six weeks'.
I hadn't even finished the statement before she yanked it off my ear and there was blood everywhere. She felt bad, helped put it back in, cleaned it and said that as soon as six weeks were up and I was healed, I would take it off. It got contaminated because of the way my mum yanked it off, I had

an infected swelling behind my ear, so it took longer than six weeks to heal and I couldn't take it out for like 3 months... Knowing this gave me an excuse to get the second ear pierced!

## "Posted on the block like a…"

Growing up, my dad used to say something along the lines of, 'you need every type of human being that society produces, the good and the bad, because there would always be a day when even the bad person would be useful'. On the roads, if you didn't know the right person/people, you would be bullied. In the 'ends' a lot happens- a lot that our parents do not have any idea about.

Back then, people were robbed daily, especially of their money and phones. Some got caught committing crimes they were asked to do by others (olders) and they did the time for it too. You also heard of people being assaulted in every way, some had 'taxes' to pay to the 'elders' on ends, which led to kids stealing money from their parents so they could pay up and not get into trouble, growing up these days weren't easy and apparently it is getting worse by the day. At age 16 or thereabouts, I remember being with three boys in Plumstead and someone brought up the idea to take the phone off some boy that was walking towards us. As soon as it was said, everyone was 'on it'. I came up with the plan, the boys executed the plan and we disappeared into thin air, later meeting at one of the boy's houses that was not far away. Soon after we all met up, I felt really bad about the part I played, so I picked up the phone, scrolled down and found the number of the boy's mother. I tried calling from the phone but it didn't have credit or minutes so I used my phone but hid my number. I put a call through to her saying that I had just found it. She arranged a pick-up, and the boys were angry, but I wasn't going to let them have that phone. I was called all sorts of names and one of the boys even tried to fight me, but they had no choice. We had to return the phone, because I think I must have said that I had used my friend's house phone to make the call (obviously I hadn't). This got him even angrier because they could easily trace his house if it got to the police. I told them that we had to take off what we were wearing and put on other outfits- perhaps dress like JJCs ('Journey Just Come') or FoBs (Fresh off the Boat) because if the boy came with his mum, he would be able to identify us. I also suggested that only two people should hand over the phone and that the others should hang around the shops casually. We got to the agreed location, the phone rang and I proceeded to the car park to hand it over with one of the boys. I can remember this so well – all I saw was a white man in his 40s jump out with a baseball bat and start charging at me! Even I did not know I could run that fast, I dropped the phone and went ghost. All I could hear within minutes were sirens. It was late on a winter evening, so it was dark. I could see blue lights up and down the stretch of the road I was on and thankfully, I managed to find an alley that led into another car park. The alley also led into a dodgy smelly corner where a lot of 'activities' would go on, I could tell because needles and condoms were all over the floor around there. I could still hear sirens. They were so loud that if I couldn't see the blue lights, I would think the police were right there in the car park. I needed to get out of that corner ASAP.

Thank God for the idea I had for us to dress like JJCs. I was wearing about four layers because it was obviously cold at that time of the year, so I took off my layers and had only a shirt and shorts on, which was random for a winter evening. I came out of the corner and into the car park, back on to the roads. I walked for about 10 seconds and I saw a police car approach me. I thought it was all over! The police looked at me and I didn't look back, I just hopped down the street as if I was rushing to the shops, even though my dressing was suspicious! I am sure it was actually because of the way I was dressed that made them ignore me. The guy from the shop smiled at me as I went past his shop, because he was the only one that knew what had just happened as he'd heard us speaking about it outside his shop earlier. I walked to my friend's house and rang the bell. He didn't even want to answer because he wasn't sure if the police had arrested anyone of us, and we were at the door with them. Eventually, he opened and I came in. One of us was missing so we were all panicking. It was at this point that I told him I had only been joking about using his house phone to call. The relief on his face was priceless. Not long after, the door rang again, it was the last guy, and he was telling us how he ran into the betting shop. His friend that worked there hid him in the toilets and later gave him a uniform to wear. As he walked out, he saw the man with the bat holding the phone in his hands and two police officers outside the shops talking as he walked past them.

This experience made me realise that I wasn't set up for that life, but I would still be friends with those boys because I didn't want to be a victim in the streets. I had later texted the boy's mum (with a different sim card so as not to use my phone number) to apologise, and she replied to acknowledge my text and also advise me to stop. In this season of my life, I came up with so many strategies to execute plans that someone noticed and said that my name from that day would be 'Skills' (spelt Skh33lz). It is clear that anyone that calls me Skills was there for that season of my life.

A lot of other things happened that I am not so proud of now, but I guess they are part of who I am today. One time, we went to FoL (Festival of Life), a religious festival. There were quite a few of us because from what I remember, we filled the top decker of the bus we got from ends. Our plan was to just go and look for girls but somehow, trouble kicked off in less than five minutes! That wasn't the plan we had we were just going to come in peace but look out for each other, no trouble! Then one person kicked it off and everyone ran towards it we moved like waves in the same direction to confront the scuffle. I remember the whole place going crazy with people screaming and running everywhere. Then before you knew it, security had jumped in and separated the fights.

I actually wasn't going to write about this season of my life, but I thought I would be doing others and myself a disservice if I didn't. While I was deliberating whether I should or shouldn't, my mum came in and told me that my family friend had just died. That was the deciding factor for me to write about this season, because he was in that lifestyle until he lost his life.

I got news of my family friend Aaron's death, and asked myself, how could he have died just like that? He had become a family man with two kids (a boy and a girl). My mum went to their house to see his mum and there were a few other people there. I couldn't go because it would have been too emotional. All I had were flashbacks of things that we had got up to. He was like me, but when I had decided that I would stay friends with the 'badmans' while also keeping my distance, he decided that he would still be fully involved. As I reflected on his death, I asked my mum how this could have happened after all the prayers. His mum was very active in her church and they had different prayer meetings for children. A particular prayer event was called 'Save My Child' it was borne out of the stabbings that were happening in London. My mum was also a regular at this event, they prayed like their lives depended on it. I told my mum that I was sure his mum would have been praying against him going to prison, but she would now rather have him in prison than in the grave. The last time I had heard about him, he was still very much involved in different crimes and was even a kingpin with foot-soldiers who were selling drugs it had become a lifestyle. What made me decide not to go down that route while he decided to stay the same? Was my mum praying more than his was? Were their prayers different? Whilst still reflecting, something my mum had said to me before jumped back at me she said her prayers could only sustain or keep me for so long. She said that I would soon have to pray for myself. I kept asking myself, did the past catch up with him?

The past didn't just catch up with Aaron. Joshua, Michael, Josiah and Chuka, amongst many others, all went to prison. As soon as I had gone to university, they literally went in one after the other for different things. Michael was first, his was for attempted murder. He was there since 2010 and only came out in 2017. Catching up with him made me reflect and I became poorly. It could have been me in his shoes (this isn't to make him feel a type of way). I remember when I told my mum that he had been sentenced for attempted murder. She couldn't believe it because she saw him as the perfect son – respectful, smart, kind, amongst other good qualities. She used to say, 'can you not be like your friend?' She didn't know what he got up to and how her biological son was actually much better. You also had some guys that got deported. Whilst in Nigeria, on a random night-out, I saw one of the guys I used to see back then on ends in the club. We used to talk but we weren't best of friends, we agreed to meet up and catch up the next day because he said he had moved to Nigeria too. I was expecting that we would have a few drinks and discuss some business opportunities he might have to share with me or vice versa. When I met up with him, he told me he had been deported. He had served some time in prison and then got deported after, it was so obvious that he would give up everything to come back to the UK, because he had life much better there compared to his life in Lagos.

# Off to university…

Who declines a university that is in the top 15 because it isn't 'popping'? Well, I did. If I had gone to the better university, I probably would have been kicked out anyway. I believe it would have been too serious for me, or perhaps I would have been forced to 'fix up'. Who knows? If only UCAS (the UK university admission service) also outlined the likely outcomes of students after three years of study! I have always been a natural when it comes to studying- I always did 'well' without revising. I got into university, and nothing changed.

When we were completing our UCAS applications for universities, we were advised to visit at least three universities that we had applied to. We were given time off from classes (I was in A-levels then) to attend these university open days. Happy days! It was a free opportunity to be away from class, so I milked the opportunity and decided to visit every university I applied to. Those days, I would have done anything not to attend classes but I had no choice than to be at the sixth form every day. One of my choices was the University of Bradford- how that came about, I still do not understand. I honestly don't know what I was thinking. I looked on the map for Bradford and thought to myself that it was quite far and might therefore be a great chance to see more of England. It was the worst travelling experience I ever had. I sat on a coach for 6 hours next to a foul-smelling man and it felt like torture. It was extremely cold up there too. I honestly do not know how people survived – I do not like the cold at all. After this, I visited three of my other four university choices.

DeMontfort University (DMU) was last on the list. It was time! My friend Ayo and I had applied together. Ayo and I had become friends at a sixth form we both attended. Unfortunately, I was kicked out for being rude to the head teacher, Miss Buddett. From my point of view, she was having way too much fun getting rid of 'problematic' students, which apparently included me. Prior to getting kicked out, I had a really bad morning. I was upset and she just wouldn't keep quiet she kept moaning in my ears about how I had missed a few chemistry lessons and how my maths teacher had also complained that I had missed some lessons. She kept going on and on, so I swore at her – 'Miss Buddett can you shut up and get the f*** out of my face'? All she said was 'Tobi, come with me to my office'. Some other students had been excluded for letting off fireworks in the common room a day before. I didn't know I was about to follow them out of the sixth form. She found my offence to be as bad as theirs and requested for my smart card – once Ms Buddett asks for your smart card, you know what time it is. After that I still remained friends with a few people from the sixth form- Ayo was one of those.

Ayo and I, along with Ayo's friend Olu (who had also gone to the same sixth form) met up for the open day. I was ready for it. I knew DMU would be different to other universities I had applied to. I had friends on Facebook that were DMU students, and had been paying attention to all their exploits. They were living the life! I knew that the lifestyle they were presenting was what I wanted my University experience to be. They specialised in the type of activities that I wanted to get busy with- PARTYING! Before my trip to DMU, I got in touch with a friend I knew who studied there. He was a well-known troublemaker. I had heard that he had been kicked out before he even completed his first year. However, he had chosen to stay on in Leicester. I planned to see him after the open day.

Overall, the open day actually impressed me. I got the chance to meet lecturers, and I met one that would eventually become my personal tutor, Mr Peter McHardy. He really sold the university to me, although I was already convinced by the lifestyle my friends portrayed on Facebook. Something else he sold well to me was the course, Entrepreneurship and Business Management. Peter spoke about the type of modules I would be studying. He also spoke about a particular module in the final year that was structured around creating a business and even pitching it to investors. This sealed the deal. I was excited about how my entrepreneurial skills would be developed and put to use (more on that soon). From that point, I thought to myself - this is it.

After the open day, we went to see the friend I spoke about earlier, as we had planned. Whenever I think back to that moment, I always feel ill-equipped to tell the story. Ayo and Olu might do it more justice, because they weren't expecting what they were about to experience, but I wasn't surprised! When we got to his flat, the environment was quite different from the student accommodation we had just been shown during the open day. My friend was sat in this room filled with some other guys who were smoking weed and staring at us. It was tense. Ayo and Olu sat anxiously in the corner as though they were awaiting punishment. It felt like at any moment, a look or even some slight movement would set these guys off. What's more, these were Peckham boys and Giggs, an English rapper from Peckham, had just released 'Talking the hardest'. So they had it on repeat and just got excited. At the time, I mostly smoked cigarettes, but I was not unfamiliar with weed. This worked against me, as Olu would end up using this to define my character- I had been smoking cigarettes the first time she met me, so when we all started at university, she would make cheeky side comments every now and then about me smoking. Guess first impressions do matter, right?

Up until A-level results day, I'm not sure if my parents knew that I had made my choice. I had chosen DMU, but they had something else in mind- they thought I was going to the 'Top 15' university. I clearly remember my mum's reaction when I told her that I had chosen DMU- she started to rant! 'Ah! What happened? I tell you to revise and you don't, and now you've ended up at a party university' (blah blah blah), like most African parents would have reacted. She was aware of the type of antics that happen at DMU- my cousins had sold me out! She carried on and on for the longest time, saying, 'instead of revising. you remain on the phone all night talking to girls. These girls you are talking to probably got into better universities!' (Can we pause please? Who remembers T-Mobile 5-Day Pass? I am actually thinking about how much T-Mobile 5-day pass 'gave me life'. If not for that, I would not have been able to talk to those girls 'all night'!) She continued to complain, but all I can remember was the excitement I was feeling. I had gotten in! I messaged Ayo to make sure he got in too, and he did. Immediately, we connected to the Fresher's Facebook groups- we were finally about to live this university lifestyle! The excitement was too real.

Finally, the time came to leave home- university time! When my parents dropped me off, I remember my mum telling me, 'I am not coming back here. The next time I'll come here will be for your graduation. This place is too far'. You would think she was the one that drove- It was an Uncle that drove all the way to Leicester and back down to London. The distance from home was a bonus for me, as I knew that if I studied in London, my mum would constantly make surprise visits. However, she broke her promise and visited me in my final year for a week. I ate well that week and my room wasn't messy for once!

My fresher's week experience was a good one. I think we went out every night in fresher's week except on sunday! I loved it- I met so many people, but most importantly, I met the circle of friends that stayed with me throughout my time at university. We didn't just have fresher's week - for the whole of first year, we constantly partied, 'popped bottles', lived, and created some great memories that have remained with me – we called ourselves #TeamMisbehaviour. My first year was pure enjoyment. I could count the number of lectures I went to on both hands! Partying aside, I had already been interrogated by the university's security team three times by the end of first year, as I mentioned in the preface. I had been given a final warning. I had been in confrontations/heated arguments, and even in fights, from the library to the city centre. The last warning was a letter that was sent to my address in London. Of course, my mum opened the letter and read it, you do not want to know what her reaction was when she called me! She first reminded me of how I got kicked out of sixth form and how the consequences went further. The things she said cut deep and it worked because it definitely made me calm down.

# Life of the party

I love a good dance- parties were my thing, but you probably could tell that by now. At one point in my life, if you were to wake me up from sleep, the first words out of my mouth would probably be 'any motive – where is the party?' We went to all sorts of parties. This is when I realised that regardless of the economic situation, people always want to unwind, so I decided, why not make money out of them?

I have always been entrepreneurial. It is second nature to me, I see opportunities around me all the time. Prior to university, I was always out partying, so I had seen the opportunity long before. My first ever party was after we finished secondary school- a few friends and I organised a party for everyone in the year. Fast forward to sixth form and I was working as a ticket rep for a team that would organise warehouse parties for sixth form leavers. If you ever lived in south London or were like me, I'm sure you would know about 'Club Nytce' from back in the day! I was a regular there too.

At university, the default for me was always going to be partying. It was the main reason I decided to go to the university, but I was already smarter and wanted to make money. In first year, I had identified the promoters and specifically noted the ones that were really making a killing out of it. When second year came around, I was made 'ACS promotions manager', which technically meant that I was to promote the ACS and make it more visible. How else do you promote a society without motives? For me, it was the permission to organise parties! Around this time, I was approached by 'Cash Buhari' to work for him. Cash was the guy in Leicester he ran 'SMART Promotions'. He worked mainly with a Caucasian crowd, where the real money was. Being black, I could relate to him and he must have seen something in me, because Cash had only worked with a few people and he was seen as the black guy that didn't work with black people/promoters. Anyway, I became the face of SMART promotions - I was in charge. If anyone wanted to get to Cash, they had to talk to me. Some people even forgot Cash was still about. I was closer to the ground (I knew what was happening on campus); I was more accessible than Cash; and also, more relatable. My first year of working with Cash was really good and the year after was even better than the first – money, girls, drinks…

Once I became a promoter, I was always promoting and running one event or the other. The only time I was able to relax and enjoy was when it was another promoter's party. We used to have this thing called 'Carnage' in Leicester those days. Carnage was a bar crawl and it was more for the Caucasian market, but Carnage was also national- it went to most, if not all of the cities in the country. Carnage was that event where we would all misbehave and not care who was watching or worry about being judged by anyone– you could be ratchet for the night, no one cared- it was an excuse to show our wildness. Every time Carnage was announced, we all got our tee shirts from the reps (the guys that owned the event weren't local promoters- I'm sure they were probably running this national event from some small city in England.) In that year, Carnage became real carnage- things got really messy and it was banned in Leicester. It was still happening in other towns close to us- Nottingham is quite close, so some students would leave Leicester and go to Carnage Nottingham. That's how much people were into it.

In Leicester, there was another promotions brand called 'Afarari' - they were the other guys that did parties that attracted our market –the urban scene. There were five of them in the Afarari camp. Cash was usually only available on event days or random evenings here and there, as he was not based on campus. Sayper, one of the guys in the Afarari camp had approached me. He suggested that we should brainstorm and collaborate on an event. I agreed and I met with them one evening in December of 2011. We had a few ideas and concluded that we should run an event that was just like Carnage but tailored to our market – a judgement-free event where you could be ratchet, wear basic non-designer clothes if you wanted to, and you didn't have to go shopping or get all dolled up (for girls). I went back to Cash and told him what we had discussed. He asked my thoughts on it and I said I was 1000% for it. Cash wasn't convinced that our market was ready for that type of event because we usually liked to show off- some would always want to book tables or buy VIP tickets- but we agreed to do it. That is how we birthed 'Barfest'.

We toyed with some other names like pass-out, shenanigans, massacre etc, but that was too wild and smelled of danger, so we went with Barfest instead. For the first event, we had planned to cater for 500 people, but 700 people showed up- we were still able to accommodate them because the venue was big enough. I approached 'Wize' of 'WizeTV' to film the event because I had fallen in love with a piece of work he had done for a friend, Mista Silva- 'It was the Boom Boom Tah' music video. The video he made was what sold Barfest. The second one we had in the summer was meant to be for 1,000 students, but then it went mad after we dropped the video and we ended up making just under 3,000 tee shirts, which sold out. From then on, it was one sold- out Barfest after the other. We weren't only selling out, but we were doing it in record time. By the second year of running the business, Millz, another of the Afarari boys, had randomly used an online tool to value the business and it was worth close to half a million pounds.

I like to believe I'm a big thinker, I get a high from breaking barriers and doing large and epic things. One day, whilst in University for my final year, I was on Facebook and saw this thing called 'AfricaUnplugged', a concert that was going to bring over 20 African artists to Wembley arena. This was it! This was the next thing- that would be 12,500 people under one roof. I wanted to get involved immediately, as it was still in the planning stages. I found out who was involved with it and booked a train to London to meet them. The AfricaUnplugged office was in Canary Wharf. When I got to the office, the guys running it, 'BadguyToba' and 'Kash' (a different Kash, with a K this time), were there with a few ladies. I spoke to both of them and told them that my market was the student market. They asked for ideas and I shared some. A really big Afrobeat artist had just pulled out- #NoAssurance – pun intended. So they asked which African act students were listening to at that time –I told them Mista Silva (UK), Sarkodie (Ghana) and Iyanya (Nigeria). Iyanya had just dropped 'Kukere' and the song and dance were catching on really quick. Toba had 'zero chill' and right there and then, he got on the phone and called Iyanya's manager, Ubi Franklin and sealed the deal- my kind of guy! I thought to myself, this is where I belong.

Remember I said that at the DMU open day, Peter McHardy who later became my personal tutor, sold my university course to me? Aside from the nightlife, the other main attraction for me was the fact that one of my final modules in my third year, 'Developing Enterprise', was fully focused on starting a business from coming up with an idea to actually going live. Also, in that life cycle, you would have an exhibition or dragon's den style event where you would pitch your ideas to potential investors and could secure investment.

When Peter told me about this, I was really excited because I never planned to work for anyone after university- the plan was to become my own boss and run a conglomerate.

Being a natural entrepreneur, it is quite easy for me to spot opportunities and bring them to life. My first enterprise was in college when I was 17. I employed two people and ran a little crèche- so many aunties had kids and needed someone they could trust to look after them, so I provided the services. I was making good money and was actually considering dropping out of sixth form and focusing on this full-time because I had seen opportunities of how I could expand the business easily. I was going to start a school pick up and drop off service too – for primary school kids whose parents didn't have time or flexibility due to working conditions- but my parents would never have let me drop out!

I really looked forward to my final year in university and couldn't wait for that module to start. Taking that module helped me birth an idea- a new business called 'Wheelie Klean'! From the name, you probably could guess what it was, but Wheelie Klean was a wheelie bin cleaning business on a roll on-roll off subscription basis. I won the award for best individual idea and I secured an investment to bring the idea to life. I later turned it down because the deal was tricky and sounded too complicated, the investor would invest all of the money as well as costs I didn't foresee but I would be on a salary for the first three years of the business and would not get dividends till year 4, although he would take his own dividend annually from year one. In fairness, the salary was twice the average salary of a graduate at that point, which meant I would live well and this was also Leicester- things were a lot cheaper compared to London.

Anyway, with university done, I was fully into entertainment. I still carried on working with Cash in Leicester and was also working with BadguyToba in London. I did all sorts with both of them from normal club nights to concerts to mansion parties. Who remembers Dominic Celaire- the guy that licked a girl out on the stairs at a New Year's Eve party after getting too drunk? That was one of many parties the team did. We also hosted many of the biggest names in the UK and African Music scene as well as celebrities and models from other parts of the world- the likes of J.Cole, The Game, Rick Ross, T.I, Omarion, J.Holiday, Wale, Rotimi (Andre Coleman in the

'Power' Series), Tahiry (Love and Hip-hop), Bria Myles amongst many others that I can't even remember.

I also started a talent management business I did this for about a year and carried on doing it on the side. My first talent was a singer/songwriter. I invested quite a lot of resources (time, money and energy) into him. By the end of our time together, we had made a lot of noise, and he had become relatively known in the afrobeat scene. He was really talented. We recorded a few songs and a lot of people wanted to feature him, so we did some and turned down a lot. Aside from featuring, we also wrote some songs for some big artists on the scene. The well-known London producer, P2J aka Pro2Jay, who produced one of the biggest 'riddims' in 2017, 'P2J project – Hands in the air', was our in-house producer. He wanted to get into the afrobeat scene at that point, which he successfully broke into after producing hits for the biggest and best afrobeat artists you could think of.

A very big afrobeat artist at that point even wanted me to move to Nigeria and join his team after I worked with him on a project in the UK, but I wasn't ready to make the move then. After the singer/ songwriter and I went our separate ways, while I was still running the talent management business, I spotted an amazing young creative who was into videography. His storytelling through the lens was phenomenal. We had a meeting, got on well and started working. That relationship didn't last three months because I had no patience and with creatives, you need a lot of patience.

## Extract from 'Misconceptions' by Debrae

*They fail to see*
*The trail of destruction*
*They leave in their path.*
*A Damn Shame.*
*Unaware of how much damage they cause,*
*Men are allowed to forget…*
*But*
*What about the woman you forced to terminate a being it took two to create?*
*What about the woman you used as a landmark for your frustration?*
*Your anger a regular visitor, your accusations a familiar friend.*
*What about the woman you shackled in a prison of negative emotions?*
*What about the woman you gave no other option but to share you?*
*Her only compensation – shame.*
*What about the woman that put you up*
*(Rent free)*
*Only for you to show her up?*
*What about the woman you strung along,*
*Even with no strings attached,*
*Only for you to make another*
*Baby girl*

*(Literally)*

*Your babygirl.*

*Magician.*

*What about the women that you slip in and out of,*

*At your convenience,*

*But*

*When the ultrasound displays your developing foetus,*

*You decide it's not convenient.*

*It doesn't*

*Suit you?*

*Excuse you?*

*What about their hurt?*

*Do they forget?*

# I love girls, girls, girls, girls....

Girls - tall, short, black, white, Asian... Just so that you can get a feel for my recklessness and understand it a little, I will share some stories.

Let me just say this before I continue - I have never been in a committed relationship, so do not judge me. However, I have had a few people that were committed to me! Apparently, when you use the words 'boyfriend' or 'girlfriend', it means you're official and you are in a committed relationship. I have never had an official girlfriend, but some people might have called me their boyfriend. I remember a female friend was speaking to me about her 'boyfriend'- she said, 'I am his girlfriend- I know all his boys and they know me too. If I were not his girlfriend, he wouldn't introduce me to the boys'. You stay there- did he confirm?

I only recently realized that I could be a caring type of guy, which I still struggle to accept at times. My first sexual relationship was at quite an early age and it was with someone that was two years older. From that point, I just carried on being reckless with females and my excuse always was- 'we all aren't correct in the head anyway- girls are crazy and boys are confused, so let's all play.' I had so many encounters. Looking back now, I liked girls too much and it was a weakness. I am not sure which I liked more- money or girls. Back at university, I would travel from Leicester to places all over just to see girls. One weekend, I went from Leicester to Nottingham to London to Canterbury, just to see girls! I had them come down to see me too. I remember a girl came to visit me in Leicester once, and when I told her that I had booked a hotel for her, she was confused. She asked me, 'why are you wasting money on a hotel? Can't I just stay in your flat?' Firstly, the money for the hotel wasn't mine anyway (for those that know). Secondly, any other girl could drop by my flat, and seeing a 'foreigner- another girl that isn't from Leicester- would be too suspicious. To be fair, girls had seen each other in my flat and they had no idea what was happening because they would usually see each other on campus anyway. I also shared the flat with three other boys, so it was easy to deny and make them comfortable enough to forget to ask each other questions or discuss. Honestly, at university I always wondered how some boys got caught out when seeing multiple people. They would have girls meeting up to discuss them and it would all get messy from there! I'm so glad it never happened to me!

I will share a story that I still find really funny. This was after I had moved to Nigeria to start a business. I came to London to chill and had limited time left before I had to head back to Lagos. I had three girls I needed to see and I had to see all of them in one day. I had an apartment in Excel, Docklands, where I used to stay at times, especially when I was in London from Lagos. That day, one had slept over the night before, so I woke up with her in the bed and noticed that she wasn't planning to leave any time soon, but I had another one on the way already!

Girl 1 decided to clean the leftovers from the food we ate the night before, the empty alcohol bottles and all the ashes and stubs from the weed we had smoked. She then rushed to the shops to get some eggs, sausages, bacon and bread, so that we could at least eat breakfast. That was her plan. My plans were different. When she went out to the shops, I packed her stuff and met her outside, saying that I needed to head off and had been called in for a meeting (easily believable because I was always in a meeting- she had first met me in one, and I was in another the night before when she came to meet me). She was really sad but she believed me, also because I booked cabs for both of us and hers was waiting. Whilst we were talking, my cab came round so I collected the items she bought to make breakfast and took it back to the apartment. I ran back downstairs, we got in our respective cabs, but I told my cab driver to hold on. As soon as I was sure she had gone, I gave the driver £10 and said I wasn't going anywhere anymore and went back upstairs to clean up quickly before Girl 2 came around.

Girl 2 came next. Funny thing is Girl 2 ended up making the items Girl 1 bought from the shops and we had breakfast, chilled and then had sex. She noticed a strand of weave and asked me what I had been up to. I had to switch it on her and tell her that it was her weave, but apparently, she knew that it wasn't her colour shade. I advised her that she might need glasses because I was wearing mine and I could clearly see that the single strand of hair was hers. I even went ahead to put it in her bag to show how certain I was, although I knew it was Girl 1's hair (but how can you tell me from a strand of hair that it's not yours?) Anyway, it was home time for her, and when she left, I was thanking God that I didn't have to force her. Girl 3 was coming after working hours, so I had about an hour to rest – that hour felt like five minutes. Girl 3 came and immediately jumped on me- she was not ready to wait, straight into action...

I wanted to spend time with her as she was my favourite. It was the last day before I went back to 'Naij', so I wanted to see the people I hadn't seen (girl 1 and girl 2) and see as much of my favourite too, but I was too tired to even acknowledge the fact that she was there. Still, I forced it, although I was half-asleep for the length of time she was there.

My default strategy whenever I needed to escape from a girl back then was to message one of the boys and ask them to call me. The boys understood this, so they would call me and say something crazy about some sort of emergency that would normally require immediate action. They would say, 'you need to come NOW! As in, NOW!!!' I would usually try to act up like I did not want to leave, but the way my boys would be pushing, the girls would usually then ask me to go after I would give them that 'I don't want to leave' speech with a sad face!- 'I don't want to leave you! You know what? I'll come back'. Have I just put my old strategy out there, or have I exposed someone else's current strategy?

There are other incidents that happened, some of which have come back to bite me in recent times. It was fun back then, but it is definitely not fun when it comes back and bites you. Imagine that the person who has everything you need to pull off a project that could literally change your life is someone you messed around with and she is not someone that understands forgiveness. Happened to me in Naij- our situation happened in the UK but she had moved there!

# White shirt gang

I was really big on birthdays. I think it started from my 18th birthday and then continued into my early 20's. The birthday celebrations in my 20's, starting from my 21st birthday, have been very interesting. I think people looked forward to my birthday more than I did. The last memorable birthday celebration I had was my 24th, because my 25th was in Lagos and I didn't have as many friends there as I did in London. (Things changed from my 26th, as you'll find out later!) My 24th was an interesting one. We had the biggest bottle of Belvedere, which usually costs £3,000 in the city! The bottle itself was a beautiful piece of art- it lit up and everyone could see it. The truth about this bottle of Belvedere Vodka is that a week before the celebration, I bought it from a local convenience store for maybe £280 or £300- can't really remember. I took it to Toba, who I also worked with. He was promoting the night and I told him that I needed to have it in the club. When he saw it he said, 'this is dope! Let's make it happen, but you will have to put money towards the bar.' I went back downstairs to the car, counted £1,000 and brought that back to him. I said, '£1,000 towards the bar and I want this bottle in the club'. Toba called the guys at Fengshui (Club Twist) and told them what I had offered. The guys were cool with the £1,000 and said that they would give me 10 bottles of Moet Hennessy champagne. Toba added two bottles, making 12.

Fast forward to the day, we all got there in our white shirts (for some reason, white shirts were the go-to look for birthday celebrations for the boys and I. Thinking about it now, I do not know why.) Long story short, I had all the attention that night. I even bought and gave out bottles of champagne to other celebrants. I remember that my friend Stephen introduced me to his friend who was also celebrating her birthday and I just handed over a bottle of champagne! According to Stephen, she kept asking him about me for a very long time even after the night was over, as would be expected, but Stephen wouldn't let the introduction happen! Perhaps he cared a lot for his female friend and didn't want me to break her heart, or he wanted to get in there himself.

Back to the big Belvedere vodka bottle: This had not even been brought out yet- it was still sitting pretty at the bar all lit up, but the attention was on our table already! Girls were hanging around and even another set of guys that had come to the club (coincidentally also in white shirts) had already found their way to our table because the drinks just kept on coming! Now the big moment of the night! You know that feeling when you're watching a reality TV show and it is time for the big announcement? The DJ changed the music, the runners (table girls) all lined up with sparklers and then they brought the monster man (the big Belvedere Bottle)! You know when everyone just stops and follows something with their eyes? Yep, this was one of those times! Plus, I am sure the DJ said something along the lines of '£3,000 on a bottle- these guys are killing it!' Everyone just kept looking over. If we hadn't owned the club already, at that point we did! Legendary moments. In fact, we didn't even finish the vodka in that bottle. The manager asked if he could pour the leftovers into another bottle for us, so that they could keep the bottle. The next time I went there, they had poured water in the bottle and just had it sitting pretty at the bar because it is such an attention-grabbing object. That bottle was there until the last day the club was open before city of London police eventually shut them down. The sad thing is that no one knew the back-story to this. I wonder if people knew we didn't actually pay £3,000 for that bottle. To be fair, we had already owned the club that night but this big bottle was the showstopper. It was a statement that said, 'Those boys in white shirts are loaded'. No one would have known that we smuggled it in! That's the problem- in this life, we pay too much attention to other people and think, 'what a life he has- he is balling out of control, I want this!' We don't even realise that it could be false. The girls hanging around only do it for the money they can see and they are tricked by the image too, giving it up and then being given up.

My 23rd birthday celebration was also interesting. I got a call from the bank saying that they were blocking payments from my card because of unusual spending and that I needed to call back the next day to have the block removed. We were wearing white shirts as we usually did. It was a very impromptu celebration, as I had till the last minute to decide what I was doing. That 23rd birthday, I gathered the boys. (Side note: I never really invited girls to my birthdays if it was a night out, because I wanted a new catch on the night! The thinking was, why block yourself by inviting 'old' girls to the celebration when there would be 'new' ones partying there? However, it's crazy that the same one you think is new is actually somebody else's old – life aye? Think about that.) But yeah, my 23rd birthday was lit. I bought my Rolex that week as well! Do not even ask me where that watch is today- I have no clue, lost it in Lagos. You would think I paid the full price for the Rolex, wouldn't you? Story for another day.

# Africa o'clock!

*"I'm moving to …(insert country- Nigeria, Ghana, Kenya, Uganda)"* or *"Why don't you move back home?"* are two phrases I hear a lot.

Nigeria, or the giant of Africa as it is called, is what I can relate to. I can write a whole book about my experience in Nigeria!

Since 2009, I had always gone to Naij in December- 'Las Gidi'/ 'Gidi' (AKA Lagos) to be precise. Gidi was the only place you really wanted to be in December- a lot of people that go now don't understand what Gidi really had to offer back then- they just don't get it, but now they have it as a constant in their annual calendars.

Due to the lifestyle I always wanted to live, I knew that I would move to Nigeria after University, but had no idea what I would be doing. I used to play with the idea of moving back to Nigeria with my mum, and she would say 'just calm down, Nigeria is more than December partying', which just sounded to me like she didn't want me to go.

When university was over, my friend Dami packed up shop and moved to Lagos. His mum was not in support of him moving and she asked him to just chill in London and leave the hustling for them in Lagos. Every time I caught up with Dami, he would always tell me that Nigeria was waiting for me- it was where I belonged and I would do extremely well there. He would say, 'I know you and you're more shaped for this market than I am.' He would also say that I had nothing to lose- If it didn't work out, I could always move back to London.

I went to Gidi again in December 2012 as usual since it was a calendar constant for me too back then. The only difference this time was that I was paying attention to every business opportunity, not only partying and 'living'. In the first week, because of my entrepreneurial gift, I had already written about 10 really good ideas in what I had then called my 'bible' (ideas journal). The one that stuck was an online grocery store idea because everyone around me seemed to be struggling to find time to go to the market but needed to do grocery/food shopping, or even when they would send their domestic staff, they would think that said domestic staff was inflating prices and swindling them. (I experienced it too with my Aunt's domestic staff and my mum confirmed it as always being like that).

I came back to London to work on the idea. Whilst in London, I was networking with people back in Nigeria. In 2013, I went back for four months to do thorough research, just to be 100% sure I wanted to do it and the market was indeed there – a lot of the time, ideas only look good on paper and the practicality is different. I completed my research and came back home to think of a moving strategy. The first hurdle was to convince my mum, so I had to lie that I was going to do NYSC (essentially a para-military service to the country) and she agreed. Up I went in 2014.

I birthed 'UncleTobi', which started as an online grocery store, then we got into the farming business and started growing our own crops to deliver to houses in Lagos. The business strategy changed to 'from farm to table'. Then it changed again to 'from farm to market/wholesaler because the 'from farm to table' strategy was too heavy to manage due to storage and logistics issues. Agriculture is an interesting one- there is an opportunity in every part of the chain. We were doing okay initially, but my lifestyle got involved and I mismanaged the business. I would go out on weeknights and be too tired to go to the farm in the morning. We had a vegetable farm of about 15 hectares in Bakatari, Ibadan in Oyo State. We grew peppers – (green and red bell peppers, scotch bonnets), tomatoes, watermelons, cucumbers and carrots, amongst other produce. We also ran an animal farm in partnership with another business. On the animal farm, we had some fishes in the water, we were also rearing snails and grasscutters, and there was poultry there too. The expansion plan we were already thinking of was to buy another old animal farm and rejuvenate it.

As I said, my lifestyle meant that I couldn't manage this myself so I trusted and gave it to other people to manage it, whilst I lived my life and just went in when it was convenient. However, 'people will be people' and they can always have their own ulterior motive/hidden agenda. Whilst I was partying and living, they were also fiddling with the farm records and doing their own thing. It was a good experience but an expensive one.

Just in case you are planning to make the move, I will give a few pointers here that I believe will help you:

- Do not be like me and make a move for the lifestyle- Is this God's calling for you in your current season? Unfortunately, when I went, I didn't even know who God was. I just upped and left because I could be my own boss and live the lifestyle I wanted to live.

- We could argue that principles are universal, as they say, but culture is what applies locally. Nigeria is unique and the laws of networking. follow-up, collaborations, etc. work differently.

- Everyone wants to be respected. In the UK, we call each other by our first names, but it is different in Nigeria. It is okay to hand over a document with your left hand in some parts of the world, but that is disrespectful in Nigeria.

- You would need to understand the business language. Barely anything is done in good will. I chased a document that I could have gotten in one week for five months, because I didn't understand the business language – in that case, the language was bribery.

- If you are planning to start a business, go there for a few months to do your market research. Most of the statistics online do not reflect most markets. I was working with the assumption that there are 20 million people in Lagos. It was during my research months when I realized that my actual target market was less than 0.5% of the 20 million.

- Packaging is the order of the day. As we say, never believe what you see! Lagos made me understand that. I had people in my estate driving the latest range rover but the flats/houses they lived in were rented. The cost of those cars would buy homes in other parts of town easily or at least pay off half of the cost. Take everything with a pinch of salt- Nigeria is the only place where the type of car you drive might determine whether you get an opportunity or not. I do not get it but seems like everyone else in the country does.

- Do you know the right people or have the right connections? Nigeria is a place where you could go to bed with nothing in your account and because you made the right connection, you could make millions in a day. It leaves you scratching your head on many things. I do not care how many degrees you have- if we apply for the same job (If you are even lucky enough to find out there is a vacancy), there are more chances of me getting the job because of who I know, than you with all the qualifications and education hours. In that example, I know someone you don't know and that person is a SHOT CALLER.

I know they say that 'tough times do not last, only tough people do' and the point is not to discourage you, but hopefully to make you understand some of the things everyone should be aware of before making the move. I have friends that were disappointed by their very own families, but that is life and that is the reality of things. It doesn't matter if you are going to start a business that you are convinced is needed or work for a company- you need to understand the terrain before making any rash decisions. First, sit down and count the cost- whether you have enough to complete it, or at least maybe test the waters before making the jump, because it gets real really quickly out there.

# Good credit or Image?

Is 'doing image' really a new thing, or is it just something that's been around for only God knows how long, which our generation took to another level? From speaking to older people, it seems that it's always been around. We all need to stop blowing money that we do not have on the things that we do not need to impress people who are trying to impress us- it is a cycle that just needs to stop.

This book is about nothing but the truth and I have accepted the fact that a lot of things aren't really spoken about because we are scared of being judged, so I have included this knowing that someone will relate. County Court Judgement (CCJ) is real, guys. I wish I had listened to people who would tell me about this back in the day. I used to believe that it was all nonsense and didn't really get it. I should be counting myself lucky that someone told me- a lot of the people I know now with bad credit didn't even know how important it was to have a good credit rating- they had no one to tell them. I had people tell me, but still didn't listen.

Growing up, we all wanted things that even our working parents couldn't afford. Even now, some of us are still too greedy and after things we know that we cannot afford. Mine started with a phone. Do you remember the Sony Ericson Walkman phone? I wanted it so badly and my parents wouldn't get it for me. My contract was linked to another phone that I can't even remember now. I remember coming home and telling my parents that I had lost my phone, thinking that my parents would go to the phone shop and get me the Walkman phone. Clearly, I didn't know my parents. They went into Argos and bought me a £20 phone instead. So I had to go bring out the 'lost' phone from where I had hidden it and come up with a lie on how I found it. This is where greed began – or maybe it started from stealing extra meat from the pot when I was much younger.

Prior to university, I met some older guys that were balling out of control and making money illegitimately. I got myself involved with them- I didn't really have a clue what they did but it was obvious it wasn't legal. I was young and they really liked me so they brought me in and I just used to hang around them. I was more of a foot soldier, so I went to university already 'breaking bread' (making money) with these guys. Right from my first year at university, when other students couldn't afford to 'pop champagne' or were popping it with their student loan, we were popping it with the money we were making. My name in first year of university was 'Sheikh IMJ Mayo'. Sheikh for the obvious reason, as I thought I had money and was balling out of control. In the first few weeks of university, I went around wearing an Arabian scarf- I honestly can't believe I did this but it felt really good then.

Second year came really quick. We moved to what was the nicest accommodation in Leicester then- CODE on Eastern boulevard- the damage to our pockets wasn't too bad. I blew my second year rent trying to make more money. I 'invested' the rent money on numerous dodgy deals and the majority didn't go too well, so the rest of the money that I had was spent on going out and living life, popping bottles and living up to the standards expected- the standard we had set ourselves to impress nobody but ourselves. The cash flow was strong, but there was just something about money at that time for me- I could not have a bulk amount of money saved up! I blew it as it came in. To think that I didn't take out a student loan but 'lived' better than most people who did! So I never paid the last instalment of my second year rent and that got me in a credit mess. The rent was a joint agreement among four of us- Ayo, Dapo, Kwame and myself. The estate agency had contacted me about the payments but I dragged it with them for a while, just coming up with excuses and thinking that once I moved out at the end of the tenancy agreement, they could not do anything anymore because they wouldn't be able to find me. I thought I would get away with it and for a while I did, because throughout my third year, I didn't hear anything from them. My parents were my guarantors and in the summer after third year of university, I came home to see them. My mum called me and gave me a letter. From the way she called me, I could tell that something wasn't right and I knew I was in trouble but didn't think it would be rent arrears. I am sure you can guess how that conversation went – 0 to 10,000 in milliseconds. I was speaking to someone about it afterwards and they mentioned a company that could solicit on my behalf. I reached out to them and was paying in instalments through this company, because I wanted to be spiteful, I said I could only afford £50 a month- what I didn't realize is that the company was taking out £35 from each £50. The third-party company was ripping me off, so I stopped, which automatically meant that the agent wasn't being paid, and because it was a joint agreement, the next letter was to everyone's parents and was about them taking us to court- that is when it got serious.

The boys created a WhatsApp or maybe BBM group (can't really remember now) and Dapo the loud mouth just went on and on. Obviously, we were friends and it was awkward for everyone the next time we saw face-to-face. Ayo was the first I saw and that was in Lagos. It was really awkward – we gave each other that smile you give just to keep it moving, but we ended up sorting it out as brothers do, with him and the other boys. I reached out and made payments to the company and the case was sorted out of courts. Did I learn from this near CCJ experience? Of course not.

Parking fines! This would have been the death of me if I didn't fix up. For people that knew me then, I drove anyhow and parked anywhere, which meant that parking fines and bus lane fines amongst others, were the norm. Some were paid, but most never were, especially the private company tickets, because they did not chase up, so I didn't do anything until I realized one had gotten me a CCJ! I couldn't believe it when I found out- I had seen a property I liked and thought that I might as well jump on the property ladder. I went to the bank for a mortgage agreement in principle and it was declined- of course the only person that was confused was me. They advised that I use one of the credit scoring platforms to find out what the issue was. That was when I found out that I had a CCJ from a parking fine. Even after the case went to court, all I had to pay was £250. I got a CCJ because of £250! Champagne money! I was buying trainers worth more than that! I could have paid it off easily if I knew what having a CCJ really meant. My nonchalant attitude and reckless living got me into all of that. Then I found out that it would take six years for it to come off my record. Six years! When I understood how much I wouldn't be able to get done without it being sorted, I started researching it and finally found my way around it. However, it will remain on my record for that period of time. In fact, when I got my job, they had to do a credit check- they saw it and asked for explanations. Who knew it was that deep? Like, for a job? Credit check? Really?

## 'Dark' – Debo

I feel so near to a breakdown and it's mental,
Tired of writing in black as if these pages of life aren't dark enough yet.
Try as I might to hold on to the moments of light,
Hoping they might lift me up above this hot air,

It seems that, as with helium,
These light moments come with their own weights
In agony.

How many times must we fall and rise before we are venerated as saints?
Look back at my walk and it's almost like a mountain range.
Himalayas.

I'm relaying the past few days to myself and I've gotten tired of complaining.
I was aquaplaning over life's landscape till I landed in a place where all I could say was,
' Give me a break."
Please!

I've been crying for help and I won't even hype like it's anyone's fault but mine
Yet sometimes I don't know what I'm really saying.
Like I died to myself,
But in the wrong way.
Or maybe the wrong place.

*I feel like a pretender.*
*When the only place I really say how I feel is on paper,*
*Writing can feel fake and the glory of the art seems to lose its splendour.*
*I'm getting tired of how dark every line I write seems to be.*
*These days I tend to write in a conscious stream,*
*paddling against the current negativity.*

# Clouds

This part of the book will really shock my parents and siblings – they are the closest to me, and a lot of the things in this book won't be as much of a surprise to them as this chapter will- they have no idea what they are about to read.

I don't know what it is, but there's something about us thinking that we are strong, or maybe we are just scared to be vulnerable. I've had different breakdowns due to tiredness, but once, I had a really bad mental breakdown (I do not want to call it by name). This was when everything went left after having spent two years in Nigeria. When this happened, I wasn't in church, so the God factor wasn't even an option. I was confused and the world was crumbling so fast- I would be in my room or car and just cry all by myself and I couldn't get my head around how I had got there – well, maybe I do know how.

Things were really bad. It was sad too because all I looked forward to was the weekend when I had an excuse to get drunk and put on a facade. I would pretend to be happy because I was at a party or a social somewhere, but when Monday came, it was back to square one. I would smoke weed and get drunk for the fun of it (it was just the only way to escape and have my mind clear of any thoughts). This was the cycle- days were on repeat. Then another addiction that came out of this was pornography. I had never really been one to watch pornography except for the random pictures and videos I would come across online. However, whilst I was going through this trying time, I would find myself on websites watching porn- if binge porn watching were a thing, I guess that was what it was for me.

After I became saved and gave my life to Jesus, I had another mental breakdown – between April and August 2017 was a really tough period for me. Usually, as you have read, I am one to get excited for birthdays, but that year, I barely wanted to do anything. My friends were the ones that decided to surprise me and do something. They decided that they would come over to mine and just chill. At this time, I had started a new venture, 'The HappyMan Media', which I will go into more detail about later in the book. I was producing 'The Heat' (one of our shows) and we decided to have a discussion around mental health in the black community. This was meant to be for everyone, but unknowingly, this was actually for me!

Everything the panel spoke about resonated with me and made me think.

Both of those separate period were really dark moments, but I was able to deal with the latter better because it was after I got saved, so I applied both spiritual and practical remedies. The constant prayers and messages I would hear in church definitely helped and there were people around me that I could speak to – I had a support system. I gradually got out of it. Now, when I feel like things are about to repeat themselves, I know what to do and when I'm not sure, I ask for help. The thing is, it is a crazy feeling you won't understand if you haven't experienced it or are not in it. You might think you do, but you really do not understand and its gets more chronic for others, but regardless of how bad it might be, nothing is new. There is the other side – this is when you come out of your crisis. The good thing is you can connect or understand when other people go through it, and it can be weird at times when you encounter people in crisis because it can bring back flashes and remind you of where you once were.

Always be ready to lend a hand when you notice that someone isn't acting normal- I have learnt always ask the second 'how are you?' The first 'how are you?' usually gets a default reply – 'I'm fine thanks' or 'I'm okay thank you', but I have now learnt to ask the second 'how are you?' This is the real one - usually, that's when people say 'I'm okay but could be better'. The later part of that reply most times means something and if they are willing to discuss, you should have a conversation and see how you can help. I was in a similar situation and when I had the conversation, the person I spoke to was really surprised when I opened up to him on what I was going through. He was able to share how he was once experiencing what I was going through and how he managed to deal with it.

For people lending a hand, please make sure you are fit enough to render help, because another thing I realized is that when people share serious or deep stuff with you and you're not fit enough, you can become anxious yourself. The heavier the issue, the harder it can play on your mind. Most times this happens so subtly without you even realising. As much as you look out for people, always look out for yourself too- you are human.

## 'Warrior' – Debrae

Sometimes,
I take
Isolated
Trips to find the root of the chaos
But end up with more clutter to add to the mind.

Pills to create an artificial high,
But end up at the hills of hopelessness once again.

Sex to forget the reality of the situation.
But after all the gasps and tugs and grasps and flicks
I find myself back at
Despair.

As much as I run
And cower behind the door of my shortcomings
It is you that I crave.
It is you that I
Really
Need.
Maybe,
It is in you that I will find the rest I am desperately searching for.

Trying to fight my demons whilst clinging onto Heaven
With my
Fingertips…

God,
I beg of you
That whilst I may have forgotten myself,
I pray you,
Forget me not.

Although it's not required,

*I strive*
*And I'm trying*
*And I'm begging*
*To be better.*
*To know better.*
*To do better.*

*But you keep me solid*
*As*
*A*
*Warrior*

*Through it all*
*With Battle Scars*

*A Warrior wandering through*
*Life*

*Striving*
*Trying*
*Begging*

*To be better.*

# The conversation!

So, this part of the book is focused on how I have survived the transition so far. The transition doesn't stop- there is always a higher level, and at different stages you will fight different battles to survive a transition. I took everything one day at a time. I did not bother thinking about tomorrow until tomorrow would come on the journey. I just wanted to manage the present day to its maximum potential. I wanted to look back each day and say to myself, well done for pulling through today. Then it became looking back weekly, monthly and now annually- it's been just over two years.

I am also not silly enough to think I am infallible or that I am better than anyone. People that relate to me know I say that a lot- we are all running this race together and we battle with different things. I might be able to deal with not having sex and being celibate until marriage, but have a bad attitude or just have negative intentions towards people. You may have absolutely positive intentions and a good heart but struggle to be celibate or just not understand the whole celibacy thing until marriage. We are all fighting battles. Although they are different, it is still the same thing in God's eyes and all we need is each other to push through.

2016. This was the year when a lot of us got tired of the norm and challenged the default. First, it was Brexit – the UK voted to leave the European Union. Ask me for my thoughts when you see me – that's a separate matter. Next was Donald Trump becoming the president of the United States of America! I had tweeted earlier in the year that he was going to win and some people said that I was mad and that it just was not possible. Just like everyone else, I was tired – my tiredness wasn't at the system like the previous two examples, but it was at my life. Nothing was progressing, things weren't happening and I felt like I had hit my peak and had started regressing. I felt like I got to a toll on a road and wasn't even sure where it would take me. To carry on with the journey, I needed to pay for the toll barriers to open, or go back – if I paid for the toll, I wasn't sure where the road would lead to. I was stagnant and saw people moving along and the only way was to turn around and go back. I was regressing – it was a glimpse of success followed by losses. It had become the norm, but just like Brexit, the fear of the unknown had gotten to me.

Naturally, as people we are happy to settle in 'default', but at that time, I wasn't even too sure what my default was because there were a few different paths for me to choose from. It seemed like default was close but also out of my reach. Default would be my comfort zone. Default would be to go back to the UK and continue party promotion, but promotion wouldn't even help. Being a promoter in the UK had a lifestyle that came with it and the financial losses I had endured couldn't accommodate that lifestyle at all- I couldn't be a quiet promoter, I would have to be visible. Also, I had returned to Nigeria to run a business and the idea of going back to promotion did not seem right. An option I was ready to go with was to run an escort agency. In fact, I had a female friend Aji, who had agreed to run this with me- she would recruit the girls and we would run it low-key and make money. It was a dark time for me- I wasn't broken but a lot of things that I hadn't bargained for were happening. I just needed direction on what was next. My business in Nigeria was collapsing – literally, except for the hectares of land, our farm van and some equipment, we barely had anything left. I needed money to come in, no matter how little- otherwise, the money I had left would be blown in no time. All of these things didn't sound right – Tobi had always worked for himself. Tobi was 'goals' for a lot of people (be careful what you wish for). He was flying up and down between Lagos and London. My first business class flying experience was at 25 with my Rolex on my wrist- I was the youngest on board that day. I remember very well- an older man even came to ask me what I did and I told him- life felt good! Maybe if I wasn't as visible and 'out there' as I was or if no one knew me, then it would have been fine to go to default.

Back to saving a sinking boat. I know I touched on the conversation I had with my mother which I believed officially kicked off my transition, but I believe that God had a plan and the transition really started when I initially moved to Nigeria. The Nigerian experience started something that later led to having the conversation.

**The Conversation:**
I remember that I asked my mum to lend me some money. She wasn't happy that I moved to Nigeria, or about the way I did it. So she didn't entertain it when I made that request. Later on, she came to the house to see me and drop some items I had asked her to bring for me. Initially, we were having the normal conversations. Then it got to a conversation about how business was going. The reaction on my face said it all- I tried to fix my face and say it was going really well. She knew it was a lie and left it at that. She then asked me if I still wanted

her to lend me some money and I said yes. By the time I said how much I wanted to borrow, she replied 'you can't have a business that's doing well and borrow that much, you joker- I do not have any money to lend you but I will give you £100 now' – I was trying to borrow £3,500.

She gave me the £100 and then said, 'Tobi, you are doing okay for YOURSELF, not for anyone else, just for YOURSELF. If you think you can leave God out of anything you are doing and be happy and successful at it, you are a joker and definitely deceiving YOURSELF.'

The conversation went on and on. Usually, I would have shouted or argued with her, but the words were hitting something in me so I just sat and listened. She then said, 'we dedicated you in the church and to God, so until you find your way back to God, you will keep going round and round in circles. Just try it and see the peace you will experience'. We had an agreement that I would go back to the UK and try God out for six months to see the difference. Before I moved, I had started going to a church in Lagos- 'God's Favourite House', Lekki- and I liked it there. I was still not convinced about going back to the UK. I don't think I have ever experienced a soul tie before so I do not know what it feels like, but I am assuming that what I felt for Nigeria would classify as a soul tie- if I go by the definition I saw on the internet. It was so strong that when I was in London on holiday, I was so restless and looking forward to going back to Lagos.

Another point she made during our conversation was that I needed to make more money immediately, as I had lost quite a lot. She asked if I was prepared to do a 9-5 in Nigeria. She pointed out that I was unwilling to work in this way in Nigeria and that I didn't even do my NYSC while I was there. Remember, NYSC was the excuse I used to get out of the UK initially in 2014 - If you want to work in Nigeria, you have to do your NYSC. I had said to my mum then, 'I have time now- let me go and get it done.' In my first year back, I had registered and had everything confirmed but just never turned up to the camp. Camp was for three weeks, after which I would have been deployed to my duty post for the year. When my mum found out, she wasn't happy. She wanted me back in London as soon as possible. Her words were 'you are just not ready for Nigeria.' I had an agreement with her in 2015 that if she would let me chill, I would apply for the next batch of NYSC which I did, but also didn't turn up for camp, so I couldn't pull that excuse in 2016.

Back to the conversation I had with my mum- she kept saying that the UK was where God wanted me to be in that season. In my head, I was thinking that she was just scared of Nigeria and its ways, so she was pulling the God factor all the time, but I decided that I would go back to London and carry on doing the things I had left behind as well as other things I could get involved in! When my mum got back to London, she would call me in Nigeria and ask when I was going to make the move. Although I had decided that I would move back to London, I was still shuffling. Then I got swindled again and finally moved back to London. We then agreed that I would find a church and start going regularly. I found TLC – The Liberty Church London.

# TLC way!

Joining TLC was pivotal- it was a major step in aligning myself with God so that he could then do 'surgery' on me. My friend was looking for a new church- he felt like he wasn't getting what he needed from his church at the time, so we took on the challenge of finding one together. He rang me on a Sunday morning calling me 'oga' (Nigerians' word for Boss, in this case used as a nickname) and said that there is a church in Canary Wharf which his sister had told him about. He said that we should check it out. I was confused because I knew Canary Wharf very well, so I checked again with him if he was sure there was a church there and he said that's what he was told. Prior to this, I could not go anywhere without seeing someone I knew. I went to this church in Canary Wharf and there was not even one person I knew. There were so many beautiful girls there. God knows me- he is actually on banter.

At this point I had forgotten the reason I was looking for a church- seeing all the girls and not a single person I knew, I decided that we had to come back, so I told my friend this. I didn't realise that he was also seeing what I was seeing, so he agreed easily. The attraction was the girls for me because we had missed the message that first week- we got lost trying to find the church. I saw it as a new ground where no one knew me and I could misbehave– just shows how my mind was wired. We came the Sunday after and there were actually people I knew in attendance. I saw four girls I knew (that I'd had something with), even a girl I met in Lagos before I disappeared. Market don spoil, I thought. They all came saying hello, asking when I had joined their church. When they referred to the church as theirs, it threw me off, as I was hoping that perhaps they were visiting. I started thinking, for God's sake! Why me? I thought it would be new territory for me- why are these people here? Anyway, this time we heard the message and it hit home strongly- I felt it, my heart was pumping. The reverse of the previous week happened- the attraction I felt was for the word and the pastor was funny- my kind of guy! If the message didn't hit home, I honestly would probably not have gone back after seeing four different girls that I knew. After about three months of attending here and there, I gave my life to Christ. I did a six-week course and I met Pastor Banks!

Pastor Banks (Pastor Bankole) is a property developer. Property development is something I have always wanted to get involved in. When I found this out about Pastor Banks, I had to network and seize the opportunity to get into it. I spoke to him and went to meet him at one of his sites the day after and he showed me what they were doing. This was the dream – still part of the dream. Spending time with Pastor Banks also helped me with the initial stages of my spiritual walk. Questions I had were quickly answered. I worked with him for about nine months and then I had to get real with myself and find a job. Whilst I was working with Pastor Banks, I was being paid, but it only covered my monthly expenses. The rest of my expenditure would come from my personal funds which surprisingly lasted a while. I also had money coming in from Barfest and from business deals in Lagos, then funds ran low and it was a what next situation.

The realness I experienced there was key in me joining. I go into more details in the coming chapters.

# Life 1.0

*'You are acting different, and it is somewhat weird'.* I heard this a few times from friends. Some even said I was *'moving brand new'*.

To become *'brand new'*, a change needs to happen- a transition needs to take place.

Transition is a space in time between two seasons in our lives. It is that period when we are shedding the skin of the old season before entering into the new one. We all look forward to the result of the transition rather than the process itself. The result brings us to a destination. We have to recognize that a transition is not fun, regardless of whether it is good or bad- changing is hard. It is a lot of work, from what I have learnt. If I wasn't intentional about my growth, I could have easily given up at different points on this journey. Instead of giving up, I embraced it! The experiences I had during my transition process can't really be explained, but they were visible to everyone around me. When I officially understood that my transitioning had started, I didn't know what to expect. I thought to myself- let me try this thing out. If it works out, it works out. This is the same principle I give to people when they ask me how I managed to just make a switch. I had given the same principle to my friends- 'just try it and see what becomes of it.' I read somewhere that you need to have the right mind-set. I do not think I had the right mind-set.

There is no blueprint for a transitional process, because we all experience it differently. I didn't have a roadmap. One thing that was constant in stories that I have heard from everybody that I have spoken to is 'renewing the mind' – which in itself is a process. I more or less winged it as I travelled down the transition path, but I was dedicated to the cause. I did have people around me to go to for advice and deciding whether to take their advice or not was then up to me. It wasn't always logical or what I believed to be good advice, so I was careful about what I applied. I just want to say this at this point- if you have transitioned from one level to another, never forget that it is a process and do not think it would be as easy for anyone coming behind as it may have been for you. Do not look down on anyone because you are now a level ahead. I was a victim of this a few times- people that were ahead on the journey would castigate me, but I had other people that encouraged me and understood the struggle-they were able to relate and I listened to them more.

Eventually, I had to say no to Barfest. Barfest was literally putting people's annual salary in my pocket- I didn't have to do anything. All we did was release the tees on a specific date and wait for them to sell out and we cashed out. I couldn't imagine saying no to free money. Before this, I had a conversation with Uche Ezichi. As mentioned earlier, Uche is my leader in church and he has had a tremendous impact on me. He said to me, 'you know you will have to stop Barfest right?' I was confused. I was thinking to myself, is this guy fully with it? However, I got a prophecy around the same time and it was clear what I had to do! The instructions were very clear: 'What you are doing now is very small compared to where God is taking you, but you have to align yourself properly.' So, giving up Barfest was necessary. I love my brothers that ran it with me, but I sat down and thought about it- we weren't bettering anyone's life with what we were doing. If anything, we were probably destroying destinies and we didn't care because we were making money off it. It just reflected our selfish natures – my values started to change.

I also had to stop clubbing. I have a friend who, when he first gave his life to Christ, would come to the club with a Bible in his hands. I thought, this guy is crazy! He is mental to be doing this. What I didn't understand is that he was in his transitional phase- it wasn't easy for him to just jump ship, so he gradually withdrew himself by doing those things and that was what worked for him. However, with me, I just stopped going because it was taking a lot from me and not giving me anything in return- an expensive lifestyle on emptiness.

*If anyone is in Christ, he is a new creation.* God's love is like no other. I was saved at a very delicate time. As I said earlier, I was at a point where I was thinking of starting a brothel/strip club type business – 'sex sells', they said. The love of money makes us do all sorts these days- the world is really a mess, looking from the outside in now. At this point, I wasn't broken but I was in a limbo of confusion and I knew it would take drastic action to recover what was lost. I had moved to Naij to start a business to make money and live the life I believed I wanted. The thing I didn't know was that no matter how much money I made, there were some fundamentals that were necessary to sustain success. I didn't know God personally, I didn't know any voodoo priest, I didn't have any altar where I worshipped. I just started a business and lived each day, so when things started to crumble, it wasn't making sense and I didn't know who to run to. Thank God for my mum pointing me in what I now know is the right direction.

I am not preaching to you or forcing a self-help guide on you. I can only tell you what has worked for me so far. I still do not have it all figured out, but each day is a chapter in this journey of life and I am not doing it alone. I have never been alone on the journey, but I didn't know that before. Now I know that God is with me- that is enough. He is all I need. I thought life made sense before I aligned myself properly, but looking back now, it really didn't make sense. I lived each day as it came- I had a picture of what I wanted my future to be, but was it God's will for me? I also believed I had it all figured and mapped out- where I needed to be at certain age, what I needed to be doing… and I wasn't even sure if it was God's purpose for me. The funny thing is, even before I aligned myself, I was quick to say things like 'we are believing in God for a breakthrough', but I didn't even know who this God was – I knew but didn't have a personal relationship with him and didn't understand what it meant to know him! Another thing I was quick to say was 'it will happen- God dey na' (basically saying God is able). I said this when I was hoping for something to happen or come to fruition. It's rather funny for someone that had not aligned himself to believe that God was able and would make things happen. Aligning myself has helped me to live my life guided by Godly values and it is making sense!

If you want to take the journey like I did, here are some things I want you to keep in mind.

## A safe house

A safe house is a place of protection- a place of safety where you can lay low for as long as you need to. It takes you away from all the distractions- it is where you run to for covering.

I am really excited about all the youth church movements/young adult ministries we have around at the moment. I think those are great safe houses for people. Find a place that works for you personally and grow there- I found The Liberty Church, and it helped me to grow and I'm still growing. For one of my friends, a fellowship in his neighbourhood helped him. After that season, he felt he needed more and found somewhere else. As long as the movement is a part of the body of Christ and making an impact in the community and in people's lives, then I think it's a great option for a safe house.

## Books

The number of books I have gone through in the past two years is more than I read in my whole life prior to my transition. Rick Warren's 'Transformed' was really helpful. TLC was running a cluster campaign and that was my very first campaign with the church. God knew I needed to go through that book and be part of that campaign at the time, because it all just aligned and made sense.

'Who do you think you are' by Dr Sola Fola-Alade was also really helpful- it was the first book I read and it was free as well because it was my 'welcome to TLC gift'. I initially went through it in two days, then went back again to read it because I was really excited and on fire- I had just dedicated my life to Christ around that time. It set the tone for the books I read next. Nowadays, I read all types of books and I pick up a new book at least every fortnight.

## Support system

You can find yourself a safe house, but you need to make yourself available too. When you make yourself available, you will have people come around you to support you. You only get help when you make yourself available and let people know what is really good with you.

Thank God I connected with Pastor Banks early- spending time with him really helped me understand things and I could open up to him. I am so comfortable around him that it is unbelievable- I do not spend as much time with him as I used to, but I am still very comfortable to go to him and speak to him anytime I need. Opening up to someone is really hard for me, but it was necessary to make myself accountable.

I also had a cluster family. A cluster is a small group that does life together. My cluster leader, was like an older sister to me. She would check in on me every now and then, making sure I was okay and always encouraging me. She was able to help me in these ways because I wasn't closed- I was open to learning.

## Accountability

I am a very private person, even though everyone sees me as an extrovert. I am an introverted extrovert- my private life stays private- I do not like people in my business.

I didn't understand when people would say things like 'you need to be accountable'. In fact, I believed that I was so grown and didn't need anyone to tell me what to do, or didn't need counsel from anyone. However, there is wisdom in being accountable. Accountability means total submission. It means 'opening up'. It might feel like you are putting your life on the line but you are really saving yourself. You don't have to be accountable to the same person in all areas of your life. You can have different accountability partners for different areas- professional, spiritual, relational (married or single), etc.

When I first decided to be accountable, I was only ready to be accountable for the parts of my life I was comfortable with and didn't want anyone involved in the other parts. That was fine- it was the starting point and as I grew and built trust, I became more willing and open. Remember that you have to choose an accountability partner wisely- some people just want your gist! They do not really care, so pray for discernment to pick the right accountability partner or the right person to be accountable to.

Accountability is a personal responsibility- you shouldn't be chased by someone to be accountable to them.

# No magic, no tricks?

The level of your thirst will determine how much you will persevere.

From the meaning of the word 'transition', it is obvious that it is a journey. Nothing happens overnight. In the same way you didn't get to where you are now overnight, things won't just turnaround in the blink of an eye. It takes eating junk food over months to gain weight and it takes proper dieting and exercise over months to lose it too. I believe that you may envision the result you want suddenly, but you then have to work at it. There is a process to everything.

The process starts with building the right foundation. For me, my process started with deconstructing the already set foundation. When I was working with Pastor Banks, I watched the builders lay foundations. There were times when they got it wrong and the cement was set already for building work to start. The process of chiselling out would then begin, which was usually a pain, because the builders had to move rubble. If they had to reset the foundation, it meant moving sand and cement from a large pile to spread over the land. Most times, they were only using simple tools, for example, a shovel and bowl to carry the sand. This seemed like a very slow process and a hard, tiring job as they worked throughout the day, in the heat of the sun or in the cold.

God promises that he will rebuild the city that is lashed by storms with precious stones. Life brings us many storms and it can feel unsettling and without comfort at these times. When we make a commitment to change our ways, that's a commitment to God to start a process in us where he can rebuild us, but this is not an easy process, like the builders and the foundation.

If we were to take an easy path and just make everything look good on the surface without the proper foundations (which was my old way), then eventually our foundations would sink. We need to allow 'the master builder' to break up our shaky foundations and to rebuild our lives – painful but worth it. This may mean giving up things we once held as important, it may mean accepting where we have been going wrong (the sin in our lives) and asking forgiveness from God.

I found a quote online that said:
*'Nothing changes overnight- I know becoming everything I want to be will take time and patience'.*

I really like this quote, but I think it is incomplete. I would add *'I must also keep taking God-guided steps daily towards the goal/ vision.'*

People see me and say 'Tobi, you have lost weight – how did you do it?' I decided to sit down, fix my diet and exercise more- it didn't just happen to me! You have to do something. Start with taking baby steps. Be resilient and trust the process. I had prophecies to hold on to- I was holding on to the word of God that is the light to my feet. I do not have it mapped out like I did before, but as I move he is directing my ways.

You will have down moments- moments where you might fall off the course. Here is an example: I have what I call daily rituals- these are the things I do daily to achieve a long-term goal. I fall off at times and may go a week without doing anything, but I understand that it is a process and I pick myself back up. Although I may have delayed or set myself back a week in the process, I get back on my feet and carry on because I am the one that knows what is at stake.

A Chinese proverb says:

*'The best time to plant a tree was 20 years ago. The second best time is now.'*

A tree doesn't grow overnight- you have to plant it first and watch it grow. Whilst it is growing, it will be beaten by the rain and suffer the stormy weather. The sun will also shine on it – too hot at times, but as long as it withstands all these difficult seasons, it will surely become a tree.

> Are you trying to build confidence?
> Are you trying to secure the perfect relationship?
> Are you trying to buy a house?
> Are you trying to be a better person?

Whatever it is that you are trying to do, just remember that it is a process. We are also so quick to knock ourselves when we make mistakes or we don't do something right. Some go as far as giving up, but we really can't. When we slip or fall on the journey, we just have to pick ourselves back up and push further. I will say this though- the process is a lot easier when you know who you are in God.

Knowing who you are in God means understanding the way God wants you to live. For me, my values started to change because there was a mind-set change.

Values are interesting and I do believe that motives behind values are more important than the values we have. Motives behind values need to be checked to assess if they are good or bad. I do not agree that money and power are bad values. Values are basic and fundamental beliefs that guide our actions. Money and power were two of my values that guided the way I lived my life. They weren't necessarily wrong, but I guess the motive behind those values were what needed to be corrected. I had to deconstruct those motives and understand clearly why I lived by them. I am still deconstructing some and this is all part of the process.

# The struggles

Transitioning comes with a lot of intensity and pressure- there are traps that you can fall into. The enemy has only come to steal, kill and destroy, and he is roaming the world looking for people to snare.

*"What then shall we say to all these things? If God is for us, who can be [successful] against us?" [Romans 8:31 Amp]*

Change is not comfortable-it is a disruption. According to the Oxford dictionary, a 'disruption' is a 'disturbance or problem that interrupts an event, activity or process.' So when my transition started, I had battles I had to fight. In the early days of my transition, I really struggled and it was because I was set in my ways, but to reach my full potential, the disruption had to happen.

The struggle was real and these are some struggles I faced:

## Popular loner

My transition meant that I had to detach myself from quite a lot of people. I had to focus just on me. A lot of people called me boring- 'when did you become this boring?' was a very common question I would get, because I declined offers to do things that weren't beneficial. If you knew me, you know I usually always had a motive! There was always something to do and people would call me to find out what I was doing.

Some people would even just call me and say to me that they wanted to participate in whatever I was doing on the weekend, without knowing what that would be. My phone used to pop off so frequently with all sorts of notifications – phone calls, messages and social media. Then suddenly, there were no notifications. There were times I would check my phone to make sure it was charged/on because it wasn't popping off. If you are not careful, such a state of being could make you feel depressed- it suddenly feels like you are all by yourself and you live in an empty world.

I am alone but I am not lonely – that was something I had to keep saying to myself every time.

## Bullying from friends

I was spitefully called 'pastor' a few times, because everything I did revolved around church. Friends used every little mistake I made against me. I could not look at a girl and say I liked her. I would hear things like, 'you are a man of God and you should not be saying (or doing) that'. Before I gave up drinking- which came naturally in its own time- when I caught up with friends and had a drink, I was bullied about it. 'Aren't you a Christian now? You shouldn't be drinking'. All these were assumptions they made, not actually things they had read or could pinpoint in the Bible.

## New level, new devils

Do not think that transitioning means you are escaping from all struggles/troubles. 'New levels, new devils', as they say. I escaped from a lot of old struggles, but I moved to another level, so my struggles became different. One of my struggles was to say 'no' to some people, and it was really a major problem because I saw them as gods. How could I say no to or disobey these shot callers? I had what they needed, but because I had transformed, I couldn't give them what they wanted or be a part of whatever they got up to. My transition meant that they were negatively affected as I started saying no.

Another struggle was lying. Lies were actually the norm for me, but when I understood what it meant to have integrity, I had to gradually give up lying. It was an actual struggle to give it up.

## A familiar alternative might present itself

Plan B for me initially was to go back to default- my place of comfort- a place I was very familiar with, a territory that I knew I could navigate my way around easily. There was a time in the early days of my transition where things weren't looking good at all and it gradually got worse with nothing good in sight. In the midst of all of this chaos and lack, I was offered what I will call the answer. I was offered a lump sum of money on more than one occasion to go back to things that I had left, but I had to hold off and stay strong. On one occasion, the cash was right there in front of me. I was tempted, I was going to collect the money, but then I countered the offer on the table with one that made no sense, in order to be able to get out of it. My offer was, 'I will take this money but will use it towards something that will glorify God'.

Instead of encouraging or supporting something that took away from people and the community in the name of making money, I was going to take the money to organise a worship experience- to gather people together and win souls for God.

The first of many abusive replies from my 'investors' was, 'Tobi you have officially gone mad! You have lost the plot. I said it!' I got home and thought, what did I just do? What did I just say? I just declined that money. The truth is that the guys wouldn't have minded losing that money if I had agreed to do what they offered, or if I had told them to give me the money to do something else- they believed in me. But the fact that I said 'God's work' put them off.

Yours might be an ex coming back into your life. Whatever it is, hold strong!

## Fear of the unknown

I think that with anything new or anything we are unsure about, as humans we will always have this fear of the unknown. After I decided to commit myself fully, I felt like I was risking it all and if it didn't work out, the shame and embarrassment would be too much for me to deal with. God knew this, because at different points, he would do things that would point only towards him and this kept me going for a while. So now, when I am expectant, I am not worried because I am in a better place and I know everything works out for his good.

**Negative energy**

So, this is different from bullying- I would rather the bullying than the negative energy. Negative energy mostly came from people that initially were there and pushed me, but for one reason or the other, they decided to start acting different after a while. Subconsciously, such things would affect you. I had said that I wanted to read the Bible in 90 days and I remember an uncle saying that I wouldn't/couldn't. I had been so motivated, but his comments took something out of me.

Also, I had a group I was meant to be doing bible study with. We started well, and before you know it, two people came with negative vibes and in no time, literally became a disease that we all caught, leading us to abort the group.

Negative energy can come from anyone. Some people don't even understand the energy they give off. For some people who are usually pessimistic, they do not mean any harm, but it is just second nature for them. However, this is harmful when you are in transition.

# Common mistakes?

We live in a generation where everything is becoming automated. 'Technology' and 'digital' are two of the coolest words around now. Unfortunately, with transitioning, it isn't automated. There is a process to it to get the right results. I have listed below a few things I believe can trip us up in our transition.

## Quick fix

In transitioning, God can give you a taster of what to expect when your transition is over, but you may run off with that taster thinking, this is it, forgetting that there is more where it came from. You get excited with the little and you forget to stay grounded and let him continue the work. Imagine eating a half-baked cake. It is better not to even eat at all because a half-baked cake would make you feel sick. I have a few friends that run to church on the Sunday of a really bad week and then they experience peace the week after and forget God for a few months. When things crumble again, they come back feeling worse. If you have had an issue for years and you think that attending a few services will sort you out, you are a bluffer. You can be delivered spiritually, but your physical/mental self needs therapy too and that happens over the course of time- you need time to heal.

## Going out too early

This is a follow-on from the point previously shared. I genuinely believe that when I went out to start the business in Nigeria, I went out too early, even though we did relatively well.

I have also had this happen during my transition. An example was when God first gave my new movement a name, 'TheHappyMan'. I literally went out too early out of excitement without getting the full picture/revelation. I did damage to myself more than anyone else because I spent money and used up favours and time that could have been devoted to something else. I was really excited. We kicked off the production side of the business- we were producing a series of shows for Online TV. We also shot weddings, but a lot of these productions never got past the filming stage. At one point, we lost all the footage we had been filming over months. If I had relaxed a bit and just started with blogging, which was what I eventually went back to, I am sure I would have gotten a clearer picture before going out.

## Underestimating the level of work/commitment

Dedication! Resilience! Endurance! Tenacity! Perseverance! All those words. I really underestimated what was expected from me. I thought that I would be a passenger on this journey and wouldn't have much to do, but I soon realized that I would have to be the driver. The car was my new found life and I was driving a car packed with heavy objects from my past. The car was weighed down and it was hard for it to move quickly. So I had to drive and chuck out excess baggage at the same time. As I travelled along, the drive became smoother. I began to enjoy the process more, but it was hard to focus on driving while decluttering the car at the same time. So I had to be skilful- I started to drive the car with both hands, and then stop at intervals to empty off unnecessary baggage before carrying on with the journey.

# Bolts, nuts & spanner

**Self – SWOT**

This might sound a bit weird but I had to do a SWOT analysis on myself. A SWOT analysis is usually undertaken by organisations to identify their internal strengths and weaknesses, as well as their external opportunities and threats. I had to be brutally honest with myself about it. I knew what my weaknesses and threats were, so I focussed more on those. My personal SWOT analysis really helped me, because when I got to a point in my transitioning where I thought I was strong enough to go to certain places and do certain things, I realised I really wasn't.

There is a part of the world where anytime I would go there, I would misbehave and my morals would go out of the window really quickly, especially in December - you figure the place out (let's see if you've been paying attention). I looked forward to going every December. I had to stop going in December because I was not ready. I had been back whilst my transition was on, but would leave within 5-8 days and would constantly be moving around. The combination of the environment and my spirit just spells 'misbehaving', and would cause me to lose ground I had already gained. It is really a weakness for me- I ask the people that live there how they cope, because I couldn't.

For some people, the genre of music they listen to can be a weakness. Mine was bashment. This music genre was something else, or maybe I was just wild. I know someone whose was slow jams. In the same way I do not understand how slow jams gets her feeling a type of way, she doesn't get how bashment made me feel a type of way – one of us must be the weird one. Maybe it's me. Bashment would give me some crazy thoughts. It is so funny how we do not know the extent to which the things we listen to affect us directly or indirectly.

**Spiritual growth**

This is the most important of the changes because the deeper I understood God, the easier my transition got. As I grew spiritually, I forced myself forward. I didn't make decisions on how I felt. It was uncomfortable at the beginning, but I got into it.

I read my Bible and I even downloaded the app on my phone. I would listen to worship songs only and pray in my car- I would just pray by saying anything that came to mind.

I began to listen to messages to help my growth. I bought books and struggled to read them at first, but now I love reading them, as I mentioned before.

After the initial six months of just trying it out, I gave myself an ultimatum to force and push myself harder for three months and see how it went. Before the end of the three months, the news had gone round that Tobi had become a pastor, not even just a Christian. I was grateful to one of my people who put my testimony on his snapchat. At that point, I had blocked him on snapchat so as not to feel like I needed to do certain things anymore. Apparently, he put up a post on snap about me and before I knew it, so many messages came in asking me, 'Tobi, is it true?' So I had no choice and just had to focus, because everyone knew by then so I couldn't turn back.

In regards to reading the Bible, the book of Romans really helped me. I still think that it is my favourite book of the Bible so far and it helped me transition well. I still read it every now and then. To everyone I have ever spoken to about 'transitioning', Romans will always be the book of the Bible I would recommend. It is very clear, flows well, and is real and practical.

A famous bible teacher, Charles Swindoll said:

*'Does your day-to-day life mirror the beliefs you hold, or do you find yourself in a constant battle with hypocrisy? Take heed of the doctrine you find within the pages of Romans, but don't forget to put it into practice as well.'*

## Mental shift

Mind-set change is the biggest of the battles I encountered. The fact is there are still so many things that need to change. Mind-set relates to the way I felt things were meant to be done and the way I thought about things. Please forgive me for saying this, but I never saw females as anything to be respected or treated specially and that is because of the mind-set I had and what I grew up around. Now, I understand that females ought to be cherished, celebrated, and adored. I understand that females are multipliers- you look after them, you do the needful and they bless you with multiple folds in return. I had to get into the transitional mind-set 'mode'- a mind-set of progression, change and advancement, so gradually, my thinking and ways of doing things began to change and are still changing. I can tell you that I have come a long way in building the right mind-set.

The mind is really where it all happens and it is really your battlefield, as Joyce Meyer said. If you can control your mind, you have won. I like practical examples- I was catching up with a friend of mine and she said to me that she used to think she was just going to get pregnant for someone, have kids, look after them and not be bothered about marriage or the man, but now she is looking forward to having a marriage and a complete family. She won't settle anymore. There's been a mental shift for her.

Another example. I was one of the people that used to say, 'there are no good women'. I used to think that all girls were the same- it was best to ignore them, get my money and then they would eventually flock to me. Coming from my background and what I knew girls got up to, you can't blame me. My environment defined my thoughts and this is what happens to the majority of us. I still have friends stuck in this thinking and I do not blame them- their minds needs to be renewed.

I know better now. I have met some amazing females and I keep meeting them. Some of these females have challenged me as a man to think right and do right.

**Some friends have to go (might be for a season)**
We all need to get to a point in our lives where we understand that we do not need our so-called friends when we need to make a positive impact on the world. The number one friend you need is God and he will send all the resources needed (including the real friends) your way.

Earlier, I spoke about the fact that I had blocked a friend for a while. I did that because I knew the influence he could have on me. If you knew me back then, you would know that I had a lot of friends and acquaintances- my circle was quite big. I was talking to a friend and he was saying that my bridal train would actually be a problem, because if I get married to someone that doesn't want more than a few people on their bridal train, I would struggle to cut people out. He didn't know that I had already dropped a few people. In order for me to align myself properly, I had to let some friends go. Some went themselves after they couldn't keep up with the new life

I decided to live. I remember someone saying, 'what happened? You just changed overnight'.

My transition is a journey, but being able to see God's calling actually took me four years of finding myself and understanding what I am actually on earth for. I had to understand that I have a purpose and that I wasn't born to be a waste or to be defined by my environment! I had to let some friends go! I had to. I was lucky that my transition really started in 2014, because moving to Nigeria had also helped to create distance from some people. With some, I had to put my foot down and cut myself off! The exciting thing is that a lot of them are now seeing God's glory manifest and they are following the steps gradually. In the past year, I have seen at least three friends decide to be better people because of what they see in me, and it is having a ripple effect- others are also turning a new leaf because of them.

When I used to be a rave promoter, I had a lot of female friendships. A lot of them had to go- I had to shut myself away from them. These female friendships came with other benefits, mostly sexual. As soon as I understood what was at stake, I had to cut them off and give up on that life, because living that life was not doing me any good anyway. I will go into more detail later in the book on how I managed relationships.

## Laughing more

You might think this is a weird one, but this is honestly one of the things that helped in my transitioning. My most used emoji is the laughing one. My most used 'word' is LMAO. I have taught my phone this language. LMAO is 'laughing my ass off' because I actually laugh a lot these days- some even laugh at me laughing. Laughter indeed is a great medicine to the soul. I even laugh more when I have tough decisions to make because it calms my soul. Maybe this was my definition of enjoying the process.

Ask anyone that went to my university, especially in the same year as me or the ones above. I never really smiled- it was a screw face every day. I would basically frown all the time and the reason I did this was because, coming from the ends, you always had to screw face so you were not seen as a mug. So I went into university with that mentality. Stephen, a friend I met at university and now a brother said to me, 'you used to scare me at university. Every time I saw you, it was always a screw face. I got scared when we would be in the lift together,

I just wanted to get to the floor I was going to and get out of the lift. Who knew you were full of life?'

Even I didn't know I was full of life. I think I came to university with that mentality that when you smile too much, you are taken for a fool. I was wrong about that.

# The gains

## Peace of mind

The peace of mind I experience these days has no bounds. I can't explain it. People see me and ask me, 'do you not have any worries?' Honestly, I ask myself too.

I value my peace of mind so much that I abstain and run from anything that would cause a shift in my peace. I do not regret the things I used to worry about. Even though they took so much from me, it makes me appreciate the peace I now experience. I understand that our experiences in life build and mould us. We all go through things in life every now and then, but I now understand that it is not about what I go through- it is all about how I go through it.

I hold on to the word that,

'though I walk through the [sunless] [a]valley of the shadow of death, I fear no evil, for you are with me;
Your rod [to protect] and your staff [to guide], they comfort and console me'. [Psalm 23:4 Amp]

I spoke about mind-set in the previous chapter. I had to unclutter my mind first and break my normal. My mind was busier than my hands were. 'Image' is something killing a lot of us and a high percentage of us know this, but we are still victims of it. I was really bothered about saving face. A lot of people saw me as the boy with unlimited resources (money) because of the way I lived. I lived a very loud life, so when things went left and I couldn't keep up with the lifestyle, my mind would usually become restless and I would begin to worry and get stressed.

The things I used to worry and stress about are now small compared to the experiences I have. With these experiences, I still have my peace of mind because I know who I am in God and I also understand now that the higher you go in life, the more worries/struggles there are, but nothing phases me. I am so confident in God that when things want to go left, I just say a word of prayer and that is it. I recently went through a dip- it was a bad time and an experience I have never had before, and it knocked me. However, within days, I was back on my feet. Before this, things that weren't so serious would play tricks on my mind for weeks. I would go from one stress to the other-they were overlapping each other so I barely experienced peace of mind. These days, the peace of God is my peace of mind.

## Patience

I'm still not there yet but there is progress. If you knew me before, you would know that I was never the patient type. I am a very impatient person. The fact is that I still am quite impatient.

I have asked a friend from University to write about my impatience:

*Tobi's impatience is one of a kind. If you don't have enough patience or a high tolerance level, you would definitely not get on with him. His patience levels are very low. Tobi and I have had many encounters where I can't stand him being impatient. He likes things his way and if they don't go that way, it's a problem. He is very used to things going his way, which is why he becomes impatient when they don't.*
*Tobi being impatient would sometimes make you fall out with him because of his delivery- this can make you hit the roof. I try my best to ignore it, as I know it is his nature and he means no harm. I have always wanted to speak to him about it. However, he is very hard of hearing and can be stuck in his own ways. This can sometimes make me clash with Tobi. He does accept when he is wrong and takes it*

*down a notch. He is a very difficult individual when he wants to be. Although he likes his own way and is stuck in it, he is an amazing person with a big heart and always goes the extra mile for others. Sometimes, he forgets himself because of others and he tends to forget he comes first in many situations.*

With the things I got involved in previously, there was no way I could be patient with people, knowing how they always wanted to pull a fast one, so I had to be ten steps ahead.

## Passion for people

I didn't realise I was really passionate about people or could ever care about people and their wellbeing. I was somewhat selfish and stuck in my ways- it was usually my way or no way due to my stubbornness.

The way I treated girls was an example. There were a few people whose love I 'awoke', but I just disappeared/ghosted them.

## Purpose and a clear vision

I honestly didn't know what my purpose was. I knew I had talents, but purpose wasn't defined. I found my purpose in the transition. I have always been very entrepreneurial from a young age, but with no clear direction and purpose to focus on. I was a bit all over the place, but in my transition, I heard God clearly on my purpose. I jumped at it early and tried to kick off and run away with it due to my lack of patience. However, I still found purpose and then I prayed for direction afterwards and things are making a lot of sense now.

## Spiritually awoken

Whilst in transition, I learnt how to speak in tongues. I engage with the Holy Spirit, my helper! This was a big revelation- knowing who the Holy Spirit is. I have become a lot more spiritually sensitive- God speaks to me. Do you know how cool that is?! Literally seeing/hearing things before they happen. It can be really spooky at times too. However, it is such a cool experience. I can't think of any better word to use- it's just really cool.

# Let's measure: Any growth yet?

Looking back from where I began, from reckless living to now intentional living, there has been progress, real progress. Growth ought to be measured and measured thoroughly to understand if you are progressing, staying stationary or regressing. I have adopted a personalised mechanism to measure my growth. It is a personal journey, but I would recommend that we all measure our lives as often as possible to be able to assess where we are.

My mechanism is called Tobi's 5D because I see my life in five dimensions. It covers the total transition concept for me, which includes both external and internal growth. Mine started internally and then gradually manifested externally.

Let us walk through Tobi's 5D:

## Spiritual

Spiritual growth is very evident. I have been spiritually awoken to understanding things of God and the way God works. I have had prophecies that might sound scary, but I am spiritually awake to understand when things are manifesting. Even in the midst of all the noise, God still speaks. I also have an active and vibrant devotional life. In my devotion, I am worshipping, meditating and praying. I am so into this that some days I have multiple devotional times and this is because I genuinely enjoy it. I didn't understand what it meant to fast- I used to think it was just starving yourself. I also thought there was only food fast. So when I was asked to fast, I used to struggle to do even half a day of fasting because it was just a hunger strike for me. Then when I finally grasped it, I began to do it for multiple days at a time.

My dreams are so precise and so accurate that it is really scary. Before, I never used to pay attention to my dreams, but now I am so spiritually sensitive that I do not take them as just a 'cinematic experience whilst asleep' anymore. I do not joke with any of my dreams- even the ones that might come across as insignificant. My relationship with God is a funny one- we have banter! As in serious banter where I laugh. If you happen to walk past or be around me when this is happening, you might think I have lost it, but I am just having a conversation with God.

## Mental

There is a serious movement going on around mental health across the world and it is a good thing. How healthy you are mentally will determine how you see/approach things. A healthy mind is something we all need. The mental shift will only happen when you have a healthy mind. Can you imagine a life worse than having no trust or happiness and fleeting moments of success that are always instantly ruined by nothing ever being good enough? It is a sad and painful story - that was me. I needed a mental shift from the default to the reality because my reality was the opposite of majority of what people saw.

My mental shift also included emotional healing. This is big because it has an effect on literally all of the other four areas of growth. It encompasses a lot- it also reflects in how you relate with people. I spoke about my love for people now- with an unhealthy mind, I wouldn't be able to impact these lives the way I know God wants me to.

## Physical

My reckless living was real. I really didn't care about my weight, in the same way that I generally didn't care about anything. Let me just say here that I am a strong advocate for people being comfortable in their body/skin because I know physical looks can be a touchy subject, as most of us have one insecurity or the other in regards to this. When I understood that there was a purpose for my existence, I knew that I needed to pay attention to my health and start to burn off some fat!

All I have done is stick to my exercise routine and watch what I eat and automatically, some weight has fallen off. This was obvious to the people that knew me. I was the last person to realise it. Then, some clothes became big on me and when I went shopping, I had to buy smaller sizes compared to what I used to buy. The downside is that I can no longer wear a lot of my old stuff that I really like because they do not fit, so I've had to give a lot of stuff out.

In terms of the way I dressed, it was all sagging jeans, trousers, pants and sliders. If you knew me, you know that I naturally had no care in the world, but over time, the saying, 'dress the way you want to be addressed' has become something I live by. I would usually sag my bottoms, but I don't really do that anymore, even though my pants have now become a bit baggy due to my weight loss and my belt needs more holes to hold the pants in place. So, sometimes it comes across as me sagging and this is a genuine excuse - but we are fixing it!

I remember I would have meetings and I would go in shorts and sliders- I have had instances where people would come to me and say, 'is this how you are going to dress to the event?' I remember Pastor Banks called me one day and said there was a meeting he wanted me to come to and he said, 'please don't come in slippers and shorts- dress appropriately!' It was a funny but serious joke!

## Financial

So if you recall, I said that I had messed up my credit and I didn't really care because I didn't know that I would need it. In my head, I was going to be rich anyway and have six private jets (one in my name, another in my wife's name and one in the name of each of our quadruplets). This was my thinking, but it was when I came out of my bubble that I realised I had to sit up and fix it. I had to open a new bank account and then find out what my credit score and rating was, and had to study and speak to someone that had an idea on how to fix it. He told me that I needed to satisfy my CCJs because he had been there before. So I made plans to do this.

I needed to save more, so I was fixing all the leaks in my finances, but I kept on getting parking fines. In 2017, I got so many parking fines that I couldn't even count them at one point. When my car got clamped in August 2018, I couldn't even argue it because I knew it was on me. When I called the guy that clamped me, he said in his meanest voice that it was because of a ticket from 2016 and that I drove in a bus lane, which sounds like something I would do anyway. In 2018, I only got four parking fines, which I paid on time – clap for my growth. In 2019, I won't be getting any parking fines (goal). Except for parking tickets, I went out a lot and wined and dined girls so that I could get with them. This behaviour obviously had to stop anyway. I think I went shopping weekly. Every time I was going out, which was all the time, it was straight to shopping centres. I also decided to take stock of my clothes- I realised I have so many new shirts that I haven't worn.

I spend on budget now, but my savings are still not where I want them to be. At least I'm now saving.

## Vocational

My purpose is clearer than anything. I have a clear purpose and a vision that I am working towards. It is not a case of maybe it is this or maybe it is that anymore- the core is established and as each day comes and goes, everything I do is aligned to it. The mystery is the process.

There is no better feeling than knowing what you are on earth for- to know that you have a reason for living and for getting up each morning. In terms of my job, I currently work in one of the 'big four', as they are called. I can tell you that on paper and with prior experience, I wasn't qualified to get the job, but God came through and I have settled in so well and at a pace you can't imagine. The perks of the job, the people I have met and the opportunities that have come my way outside of my core job are absolutely unbelievable. I can also say that I am on a 9-5 in purpose (I elaborate on this later in the book).

# The secret ammunition!

To summarise this particular transition season in my life, I can't think of any other word than 'intentional'. My secret has been living intentionally ever since I understood what that meant. I came from what I will describe as reckless living and have arrived at intentional living.

I hope that from my writing, you are inspired to be a better person for yourself, your family, your community and for the world as a whole. The world is currently too dark and it needs you for a change to happen, but before the world changes and becomes better, you will need to be a better version of yourself first because you are the one that will make the change happen.

I decided to fix up, do more with my life and make my life have meaning. I wanted to be relevant/known for the right things like making positive changes in my community and making the world a much better place, which are amongst the good intentions that most of us have. The one thing I had to learn is that these good intentions needed me to act in order to make them a reality! The only way this was going to happen was for me to be intentional about my good intentions. If you automatically think that as you increase in age you will naturally grow, you are right in terms of physical growth but you would still have a child's mind-set.

Personal growth, which is what I like to call the real growth, is the growth that happens internally and requires a lot of hard work. Internal growth today is the only guarantee that tomorrow will get better.

A common excuse we all tend to use or the easiest thing to blame is always the system. The system doesn't support your good intentions most times, so you have to push. People will say to me, 'I do not need a spiritual awakening to get that'. That is true but I can only tell you what has worked for me and my religion is the main thing that has helped me deal with the extras. The extras are the distractions such as the system, my environment and my culture, because these are the things pushing against my intentional living and it is so easy to give up without something backing you. For me, this is where the God factor comes in. With God behind you and you submitting to his ways, things are a lot easier.

The work is easier because although work is still required, it is with less effort and you also understand that your standards aren't defined by those of the world but are defined by principles guided by faith.

## What does it mean to be intentional?

It means you are purposeful in word and in action. You live a life that is meaningful and fulfilling. You do not make judgements based on what the world says is right. It means you make thoughtful choices in life. You are actively engaged with your life and you truly interact with yourself- you don't deceive yourself and you do not live a 'fake it till you make it' lifestyle. You take rejection as what it is and don't reply with bitterness. You wake up every day and in every situation and you ask yourself, how am I going to make the most of this opportunity to still be alive, as clearly, God is not done with me? Every day is an opportunity, because tomorrow isn't promised. I would go further and say that even every breath is a blessing that we should all be grateful for.

If you truly want to live intentionally, you need to understand that every decision you make directly impacts your experiences. So decisions should be made rationally- repercussions should be thought of thoroughly before actions. These days, before I make a decision, I take it through my personal 'culture vs principle' test. My principles are all faith-based so they are not just things that I have randomly thought of or just random beliefs that I have pulled from the cloud. After my culture vs principle test, I then make a decision.

Living intentionally means that you have control over your mental, emotional, spiritual and physical well-being. It means freeing yourself from self-limiting conditioning. It requires gaining clarity about what you want, who you are, owning what you say, as well as choosing how you 'show up' in all situations and how you want to contribute.

Do you wake up every morning ready to face the day? Are you generally happy? Do you feel engaged and excited to live your life? These days, I do- my life isn't perfect and yet my life is great! My day doesn't always go the way I want, but I learned long ago that getting my way isn't the secret to loving life. The secret is living intentionally.

## Why be intentional?

Be intentional because you want to do more than just get by. I spoke about going back to default earlier. That would have been me just getting by. Another example of me just getting by was when I was working for Tower Hamlets council before I got the job with PwC. I could settle and be comfortable in what I was doing, but I had come to the realisation that I had a purpose to live for and my purpose was more than an administrative role in Tower Hamlets council. I was intentional about that change and God did the rest.

Be intentional because you dream and a dream doesn't come to reality by just coasting, which is what we tend to do. I heard God clearly about this book and making it a reality required me to be intentional, or else it would have been an idea that never came to life. When it came to dating, I knew I wasn't in the right mind-set. I needed to understand the basics, so intentional living required me to focus on me and becoming a better person rather than dating and causing more damage. When I understood things better, I was then able to go out and date purposefully. It was also easy for me to identify time-wasters and potentials.

I am upfront with people these days. Even though the conversations aren't the easiest, I have to have them – intentional living! Sure, it's easy to do what the culture supports, but with intentional living, most of the time you do the opposite.

## How to be intentional in all you do
### What is important to you?

I needed to decide what was important to me- was it the following on the 'gram; coming across as smart; having a wealth of information in a world full of a lot of lazy people that consume anything brought their way; or was it me actually becoming a better person so that I could then pour myself into others? Definitely the last.

I knew what was important to me and what still is, so I took time to work on me and become a better person. I focused on the version of Tobi 2.0. Anything I do now is kingdom-focused. Will the right people be proud of me and ultimately, will God be proud of me? That is a question I always have at the back of my mind- he who is faithful with the little will be given more.

**Be true to yourself**

I remember about a year into my transition, I had an opportunity to speak at an event for young people around submitting themselves to God and letting God do the rest of the work. This was a good opportunity for me to post on the 'gram, but I knew I wasn't ready for it. I knew I was still understanding some basics, so I declined the opportunity. I didn't do it for the 'gram as most people would do.

I go online these days- I see people with so much following but no content and they are polluting people's minds. Initially, I was quick to blame the listeners: Don't they know what is right from wrong? Can't they see that everything they are being fed is going to damage them in the long- run? Unfortunately, with where the world is now, a lot of people are trying to find their way, so these people pouring out their information have a ready market of vulnerable people. I could have taken that opportunity and spoken at the event. I would have probably gotten a few people come to me after to say, 'thank you for that, it really helped me', but I knew that it was half-baked information and I was not ready to worsen anyone's situation. These days, when I get asked things that are beyond my understanding, I point people in the direction I know they can get help.

**Accept your imperfections**

The general assumption in life is that as you get older, you know better and naturally become better. This is a very big fat lie we all tell ourselves. Another lie that I have heard is that imperfections will go, and we will become 'perfect' naturally as we get older.

Well I know you have to strive towards perfection – but does perfect exist? Imperfection can be physical or can also be personality shortfalls. Regardless of which category yours falls under, always remember that you are enough the way you are – we love your fat nose, your beardless face, your fat face, your complexion or your small boobs. We understand that even though you are trying to work on yourself, you may sometimes still get annoyed easily, or show up late to things. Just keep working at it!

Imagine if God made us all 'perfect'. What are the chances that we would need his help? He made you the way you are so that you can also do your part and keep becoming a better version of yourself. I have accepted myself the way I am and I am continuously working with intention to get better. Human beings mostly focus on external beauty, but have you ever met someone with a beautiful soul? This for me should be the focus, not trying to perfect the external whilst the internal is still filthy. If your inside is filthy, no matter how beautiful you are externally, it will always be exposed for people to see.

**Be creative and open to options/choices**

With intentional living, you have to be open and remain positive. A lot of us are stuck in our ways, habits and attitudes. I was the 'my way or no way' kind, but I had to understand that if I was truly about being intentional in everything I was doing, a lot of the things I believed in would need to be binned. It wasn't working anyway so why stay stuck in those ways and beliefs? I had to open up to trying things out in different ways and hope for the best results. My relationship with people has experienced a lot of progress because even though I thought I was a people's person naturally, I came across as a user to a lot of people as I had been all about myself, and they then pushed me away. So it is not about what I am getting from a relationship now- there is a balance. I am pouring into the relationship as much as I am taking.

**Declutter your life**

Why carry baggage? When it is only occupying space and holding you back. Get rid of the habits, attitudes, situations, and people that you don't fully embrace. Rid yourself of those things that hold you back from living a purposeful life. If something doesn't have meaning or value in your life, if it all it does is take away from you and doesn't add anything, why hang on to it?

**Forgive**

Forgive yourself and forgive others for past wrongs- those things are in the past. Holding on to resentments holds you back.

**Live in the moment**

Life isn't only lived when you get the raise you deserve, have the car you always wanted, or find love. Life is lived in this moment. Enjoy what you have here and now, not what will be in the future. Enjoy what is today.

**Stop worrying about everyone else**

It doesn't matter what anyone else is doing. What matters is what you do! It doesn't matter what anyone else is thinking.

What matters is what you think about you because you know who you are in God!

I know this might be a common concept we hear a lot, but it is really powerful if we can grasp it- the people that we are trying to impress (our distractions) also need help and in most cases, they are probably too busy wasting time focusing on their own distractions rather than seeking help themselves.

I had a conversation with someone that had a real influence on me and it made me realise this. When he spoke about his own issues and struggles, he said he had begun to use my life as a model and this gave me a deeper understanding- all that matters is living for me rather than others.

**Keep living the good life!**

The good life is the life you live today. It will determine your life 10/20 years from today. Live it today and do it again tomorrow. Keep practising. Keep learning. Keep exploring. Keep thinking. Keep choosing. Keep living. Be intentional in all you do!

**Make a commitment to grow and make it public**

When I became a Christian, I did a testimonial video to let people know that I had decided to live a better life. In the video, I highlighted some of the things I have said in this book. The video then went viral, as I have mentioned before. When I was initially approached about doing a 'transformed life video', I wasn't too sure about it, but because I had a commitment to grow intentionally in myself, I thought, why not? This will help more- it will also help me to be accountable to more people. It did come with some backlash, like people whose opinions didn't matter now thinking they could judge every single mistake I made. Some people that I didn't know suddenly thought they knew me and would later go on and tell people my history – not sure what they were trying to achieve doing this, but these are some of the consequences you might not have bargained for. Making it public really did help, because I became more self – aware. I wouldn't just rationally do things all in the name of 'YOLO' or not caring. I had second and third thoughts about things.

The video itself wasn't enough, but it helped. A few others did the video too and they have reverted to where they were coming from- it needed my commitment to become the perfect formula.

**Journal, review and act**

I painted a picture of the life I wanted and broke it down into years- the changes I wanted to see and where I wanted to be in one year, in 5 years, 10 years and so on. It included quite a lot of things such as having a family (my wife and the quadruplets I wanted, as I mentioned before). Maybe this explains why I am still single- every girl thinks I am crazy when I say this and they are quick to ask, 'who is getting pregnant, you or your wife?' I say that it would physically be her but that we would both be carrying them

I have taken this picture I painted of my life to God in prayer- let his will be done. This helped me understand what I needed to have stopped doing by when and what I should be doing by month x. This really helped me declutter my life and have a focus. I set milestones and at each milestone, I do an honest review. I didn't try to declutter or become better in every area of my life at the same time. I focus on an area at a time and develop skills. An example was that I gradually stopped going out all the time and developed a genuine love for reading, so instead of going out all the time, I would be indoors reading.

I invest an hour a week in reviewing my week now. I journal as I review. At the end of every month, I go through all the reviews and pick the highlights or concerns that I need to pay attention to. I have a folder on my laptop dedicated to this so I can go back at the end of the year and reflect on the year!

**Share your growth and pour back into someone**
Sharing your growth is not to make you look superior or better than anyone- it is a motivator for me to keep pushing and to do more. Make sure you are sharing with someone who genuinely cares. They do not have to be a friend or peer of yours. I know people are quick to say, 'surround yourself with people doing better than you'. I would say, surround yourself with everyone- both people doing better than you and people that are not doing as well as you are but are willing to get to where you are- this will also spur you on.

I have a few different stories of when I have shared my growth with people, but I will use Adeola as an example. When I first agreed to mentor Adeola, an undergrad from Wolverhampton University, I was excited. We started the relationship and I saw how much she grew in the short time we spent together. I think it was at our second meeting that I asked her about boys.

She was shocked- the mentorship programme was only to help when it came to a career and securing a job after university (which God made happen). That's what it says on paper, but I was more concerned about her total wellbeing than just her career life, which includes her relational life too.

Mentoring her meant I could help her become a better person all round, which she did. By the end of the year, she had secured a few engagements for herself both in the UK and abroad. She is getting ready to produce her first documentary and is now really passionate about young females and their struggles, which is beautiful to see.

Seeing this reminds me that I cannot afford to fall off or slip up because, now with the help of God, I have managed to help this young woman do more and go for every opportunity available to her. When she sent me a picture of her at a recent Labour Party Conference, I was really proud of her. She took pictures with quite a few notable Labour party leaders- these pictures got me thinking about my next move on this journey. I remember I was going to sleep when I received the picture. As you can guess, the plan changed so quickly from sleep to finishing my website and starting the plan for my TV Show. I had pushed these two things back for a while, but those pictures spurred me on and for motivation, I sometimes look at them just to remind myself of what is possible!

Pouring back into the community by improving someone else is not for show or for you to get accolades- it helps you too. It is beneficial for all parties involved. It reminds me of my commitment to live intentionally and also motivates me and helps me stay on track.

## *Friends for sale –Ekae Longe (Inktippeddreams)*

The pawn men asked me why I came,
I held no trinkets to be sold,
I looked down at the floor in shame…

"Do you buy only treasures and things?"
He wasn't quite sure what to say,
"Well dear, it's whatever the customer brings…"

"Then I have some strange goods to sell".
I held out some of the friends I'd made,
"As you can see, they are packaged quite well".

"Whatever's the reason to give them away?
It must hurt to let them go"…
"Well, they are kind of in my way".

Mr. Pawn Man's face showed disgust,
The same brand I'd felt too,
"Why have friends you can't even trust?"

I was glad he could now see.
"So how much would you want to pay?
I'm willing to let them go for free".

"Well, my dear, it really depends,
They need to have some sort of use,
Since they are no good as friends."

"Can they pick good places to eat,
And form good chats on headline news?"
I was really quite amused…
"Yes, Mr. Man, that's their only feat."

*So there and then the deal was made,*
*I gave my friends to this lucky man,*
*As I walked away, I let their faces fade…*

*"Aren't you scared of walking alone?"*
*Mr. Pawn Man asked as I went,*
*I guess this was a way to vent…*
*"That is what I have always known".*

# Managing people in my grey years

Naturally, I am not someone to cut people off - in fact I still do not know how to do it. So, before my transition, I had all types of people in my life. This saying is so valid: 'The people in your life can be either your biggest asset or the biggest curse'.

When I became a Christian, I knew right away that if I really wanted to do it properly, I needed to manage all my relationships rightly, or else I would find myself doing the same things I had left behind. Before I became a Christian, a friend of mine who had moved in the same circles had become a Christian and I saw the way he dealt with things. Some people think my change was swift, but Michael's was drastic. He was so tough on himself that he wouldn't reply to messages about going out or 'misbehaving' (so to say). Strangely enough, he was always ready to go to weddings (that was his release valve). Maybe it explains why he was the first of the lot to get married.

Early on in his walk, he found a girl in his church that later became his girlfriend and then his wife. So she more or less took all of his time anyway and he was focusing on that. Things happened really quickly for him. While we were still gallivanting and getting up to all sorts, he was already planning his wedding. I believed it worked out for him because that was what kept him occupied, but prior to this, he had already stopped coming out and he was firm. He got rooted in his church community and got actively involved, so he had limited time to link up.

I applied Michael's strategy. Well, some part of his strategy. I didn't get into a relationship. I needed to understand what it meant even to date someone, not to talk of being in a romantic relationship. Michael had been in committed relationships, so he knew the fundamentals. I hadn't been in one. I had seen people without any commitment from my end at least, so I had a lot to learn. In hindsight, that decision made sense.

I became rooted in my local church. I literally signed up for everything and anything I thought I could help with. I joined about four interest groups (groups that share common interests or goals)- I joined 'football'; 'bible in 90 days'; 'business and every man's battle'; and 'winning the war against sexual temptations'. Boy, I needed that! I also joined a cluster family, as I mentioned before. All of these were in order to keep me grounded and less distracted so as not to be influenced. I was still distracted, but I was cautious about not letting those distractions get the better of me.

Influence can come from anywhere, but for me, my friends were more of the influences directly (physically) and indirectly (their virtual lifestyle). You need to understand who you are in any relationship- are you the leader of the pack or are you just a follower? You need to have a very honest conversation with yourself- how easily are you influenced? Or are you the one that influences everyone else in the circle? I know we all have different relationships with different people. The relationships where you are the influencer are easier to manage. With these relationships, you may not need to distance yourself from the other parties because you have influence on them. You can say 'no' comfortably as they look up to you (so to speak), but you would still need to watch closely and be careful, because in subtle ways, even these people can influence you. An example- a guy I know found out how to make money illegitimately and he came to tell me because he knew I could source what was needed. He was a guy that used to work for me, so I told him that I would get back to him. I never did and then he found the resources himself. He then came back to tell me he had done it and let me know how much he was making weekly. On some level, I was considering it, so I had to tell him and others like him not to bring such things my way. He respected that and didn't speak to me about anything that he knew was inappropriate. It was easier to do this because I had influence over him.

For relationships where I was not the influencer, these were the tough ones to deal with. They can become quite toxic if you do not manage them well. I remember a friend trying to dissuade me from becoming a Christian- he said this to me: 'guy, I have been there, there is nothing there for you and all is just package'. This is negative energy. At least his approach was direct whilst someone else's might be more subtle and you wouldn't even realise. He might not have meant to be negative because that could have really been his experience, as the statement was borne out of his own personal journey. However, because I was making a positive decision, I would have expected him to at least encourage me. He could then maybe share his experience after, but then help me understand that the journey is personal and his experiences don't dictate mine.

A real friend would respect your decision and hope for the best for you, as long as it is a good decision and there is no harm in it. My friends at that point were a very interesting set of people. This was the time I also realised that a lot of us throw the word 'friend' around too easily- a lot of our so-called friends are not even loyal to us. One thing I continuously do is check the circle of people I call friends and constantly categorise them.

Just to illustrate how wild some of my so-called friends were, I had friends that would send me nudes of females they were with. A message would drop on my phone- it would be a picture of a naked girl and the next thing they would ask me is if I wanted to come over- 'she is here with her friend'. In some cases, old flings would send me nudes saying directly/indirectly, 'I am sure you miss me.'

I had friends sending pictures of money they had just made and the new luxury cars they were driving. These were toxic relationships because they were going to frustrate my newly-made decisions if I didn't do anything about them. I really struggled in my earlier days- I still have my struggles, but I can manage them better now. The only solution was to be tough on myself. I had to put things in place to protect myself, because I come first and I am the one that matters most.

I had to have conversations with some people and let them know where I stood on certain things. These were polite conversations and a lot of people respected what I was saying, but some people laughed at me. Some others even thought it was a strategy for something else I wanted to do. I remember a female friend thought it was because I found a girl in a church and I was doing it just to win her over. I can't blame her because I had once walked a girl I met on the bus all the way to a weird location that was supposed to be a church so that I could talk to her. I then deleted her number as soon as I found my way out of the 'church'.

A friend was telling me how a guy really liked a girl and made his move but she said 'no' based on advice from her friend who told her that he wasn't good for her. They moved on from each other, only for him to get with the friend that had advised her. He proposed to that 'friend' and they got married within a year of his proposing. I believe in fate and God's plan, but that still shows how friends can be. Not everyone wants to see you happy. You come first and then friends after- it is good to seek counsel, but who are you seeking counsel from?

I digressed a bit, but just wanted to show how friends can be. Friends need to be controlled rather than having them control you. I was intentional about my change and new walk- I had to establish clear healthy boundaries with the toxic relationships I had, as they were not going to respect my new way of life. Aside from that, I didn't put myself in situations I knew would be tricky. Healthy boundaries meant that no one would lose out- I would do my thing and so would those friends. There was no bad blood, but they just could not reach me at that time. My blocked list numbers increased and I did some unfollowing too.

Except for the relationship boundaries, I also set myself some personal boundaries with people. These boundaries varied depending on the category of the relationship - it is just what I had to do for me. We are humans at the end of the day- we are flesh, so as much as your friends can be the problem, also check yourself and guard yourself.
Here are some of my personal boundaries:

### Guarding my environs
I put a pause on my annual Christmas trip, as I said before. If I kept going, I would have been opening a big can of worms.

There was also this thing about 'fear of missing out'. It was tough not to go in the first year, but a lot easier in the second and third year. In the first year, I didn't go and didn't watch anyone's snapchat stories, but it was still tough because my mind was there. In the second year, I watched snaps and still felt some type of way but consoled myself that at least I was saving money (see the positives right?)- so, not as bad as the first year. It was difficult, but I had to do what I had to do and when 2018 came, I didn't even think of it.

**Taking care with group holidays**
I stopped going on group holidays with some people. They still message me to ask if I would want to go. These are places I would love to visit, but I know that being around this particular set of people is already tricky in London. At least, when I'm here, I can grab my car keys and go home if I feel a certain way, but going abroad wouldn't be as easy. 'You could just go back to the hotel right?' – Easier said than done.

## Taking care with social media

Snapchat, Instagram, WhatsApp. I call all these things the market place. In the market, you have all types of people. I believe we can all relate to this one. Apple's screen time is a real game changer because it breaks down the time spent on all these apps for you. The less time spent on them, the less junk you consume?

I have a friend that deactivates and deletes all these networks frequently. Usually every Monday, the apps are all gone and then she has them back for the weekend and deletes them again by the time Monday comes around. I didn't go that far- I just blocked and unfollowed people. My timeline wasn't popping so I gradually stopped going on there as frequently as I used to. I have been more active of recent because I know my mind is healthier and I can deal with things differently. I still find WhatsApp the most difficult, but it's apparently the easiest for most people.

## Having firewall friends

My firewall friends - these are my real Gs. Firewall is meant to protect you from unauthorized access. I have both male and female firewall friends. My friend Lape was one, even though she could be annoying at times. The irony is Lape and I weren't friends initially. In fact, she was sceptical about me because of what she heard, but our friendship developed. Lape would literally hang around me and any girl she saw me speaking to for too long. I could easily get carried away and would start laughing and saying things I shouldn't be saying, but once I saw her around, it was a reminder in my head- fix up. On a few occasions, when the conversation would get to 'let's exchange numbers', Lape would step in and give her number instead.

A few times, I would want the number because the girl was good-looking, but to protect the grounds I had covered and to keep growing, Lape was the firewall. A lot of my boys who are around me these days are also firewall friends. I feel like I am the most unserious one of the lot now- they look out for me and have their eagle eye out. There are situations where I haven't been sure of how to deal with things- I speak to them and I take their advice because I believe what they say.

## Our new language - emoji

This might sound weird and ridiculous but remember this is personal.

We know they are basically word substitutes- you can have a conversation/pass your message across with just emojis. A lot of us have- we know ourselves! In my recently used emojis, you wouldn't find the kiss, love-struck or any of those obviously flirty or suggestive emojis. I know myself and my cheeky nature- I know what I could do with those things, especially when it came to my relationship with the opposite sex. An example- my default response when someone would send a kiss was to reply saying, 'I would prefer a real one though'. That statement would take the conversation to another level a lot of the time. So, when people send kisses now and I do not reply with one, I am sure that majority of them think I am rude or not feeling them like that, and it gets awkward at times.

## Having mentees

I have mentees that I am helping to grow and develop to become better people in their five dimensions of life. The growth is also not only for them. In fact, I am learning more about myself and how to deal with people. Just the thought that I have someone looking up to me keeps me on guard. I am human, I know that, but it scares me to think that all these people are looking up to me and I could mess up.

To conclude, relationships are the most important resource to man. They make or break you, so you have to choose carefully who you associate yourself with. They can be the biggest blessing to man or the biggest curse also. You need to understand yourself, categorise the relationships in your life (including relationships with family), and for the toxic relationships, if you have to cut them off, do so. When the results pay off, they will all come to you for help or advice. I have now learnt that there is nothing wrong with cutting people off for a lifetime or for a season, because you need to grow. There are also times you have to run- run for your life and keep running. I thank God I didn't have to change my number. I only got my current phone number about a year before I became a Christian, so not a lot of people had the number anyway. A friend of mine had to change his number. He knew that keeping the number he had wasn't helping because the toxic people could still contact him. So he got rid of the sim card and got another one- it was painful because he had only just renewed his contract about four to five months prior, so he had to pay the difference. It wasn't cheap, but he was intentional and tough on himself and knew that was what he had to do.

# You are not alone - #MeToo!

*'Let your light shine before men in such a way that they may see your good deeds and moral excellence, and [recognize and honor and] glorify your Father who is in heaven'. [Matthew 5:16Amp]*

God is ready to use you as you are- you just need to align yourself. Nobody is too young or too old to align themselves. Your help isn't coming from anyone. You have to help yourself and God will do the rest.

'I look up to the hills. From where cometh my help? My help cometh from the Lord most high' - You have to look up. Looking up is not just the action- it is actually a lot of work and requires serious commitment. There is nothing new under the sun. Even the Bible says it.

*'That which has been is that which will be [again], and that which has been done is that which will be done again. So there is nothing new under the sun'. [Ecclesiastes 1:9 Amp]*

We all have individual stories. As I have shared, I was involved in all types of mess. No mess is too much for God to sort out. Life happens to everyone and whatever you might be going through is all a set-up for the more glorious and bigger things that will happen to you.

Life is a set-up, but there is an awakening- one thing leads to the other. I think it is just God's sense of humour, almost as if he enjoys having banter with us at times. He lets us do our own thing, feel the repercussions, and then, an awakening happens. An awakening is like a light bulb coming on- it's a wakeup call. Life is so funny- some people are lucky and do not even experience any repercussions, whilst some others get hit really hard. Some feel just a fraction of the hit before their awakening. With the mess most of us have been through, I doubt there are any new scenarios of the life lived before the awakening. Even if it is a new scenario, yours can't be the worst. I have had people share some serious stories with me- both theirs and others- which has helped me realise that everyone has their own battles.

When the awakening happens, will you be responsive? Our life experiences are different, so our awakening experiences won't be the same. I honestly believe you could miss it. I know some people believe God will always be available and that there is grace. They believe that you can go and 'do you' and just come back to him. God is gracious, but a lot of times, the things we do now don't manifest right away because they are like seeds sown that would eventually grow into weeds. They manifest in different ways such as regrets, pain, loss, tough lessons and heartbreak amongst other not so pleasant things. Further down, I will share some experiences that people have shared with me. I hope they encourage you and that as you read this book, you experience your awakening- that is, if you haven't already experienced an awakening.

Our past shouldn't define us. We all have stories to share and I think we all need to be more open and share those stories. The world is too dark, so we ought to be light in this dark world. Light is essential- have you ever been in a situation where you know that you are looking really nice and wearing a really nice outfit too but the lighting everywhere you go is really poor, so you can't take that one picture for the 'gram? That frustrating feeling! Then as soon as you find the perfect lighting you are excited- that is the power we should all carry. It is the power we all carry, but we just need to let our light shine.

Imagine how beautiful the world would be if we all lit it up. Have you ever walked into a store that sells chandeliers or light fittings? They are always really beautiful. Or have you been to those event venues that have amazing lights? Imagine how grand that looks! Now, imagine the world we live in as these venues or stores. Do you know how beautiful it would be? We need to see our world literally lit up like those places.

My awakening wasn't due to being broken, although I realised after my awakening that I was really broken and a lot of fixing needed to happen. Some of that fixing is still in progress. My awakening came after glimpses of success but with nothing really to show for it. The success was obvious to everyone, but I knew there was a void. The sad thing is that people saw how I lived and there were people wishing for my life without really knowing what they were wishing for. They believed the virtual life I lived. What it took was for my mother to say, 'the only thing missing in your life is God- you need to retrace your steps back to where you were dedicated, which is the church'. At that point, I could have ignored her and carried on with life. To be fair, I would most likely be fine. I would live life but in emptiness, knowing there was a void in me that needed to be filled.

That awakening means it is time to rewrite your story. Here are some stories shared by my friends:

Sandra was totally broken. In her words, 'I have aborted numerous times and had crazy sexual escapades with all types of men', and she blames it all on her daddy issues because she tried to find security in boys/men. You might think it's a silly excuse but you are not in her shoes so you wouldn't understand. I saw her last year and she was running a female empowerment/mentorship scheme for young girls. I was shocked, and after speaking to her, she had become an entirely different person. I was confused because she was what you would call the 'local slag' on ends because of the things she got up to.

She was a top dog and brought other girls in. Half of those girls still have their lives all in a mess but she is out of it after being responsive to the awakening. She has tried to bring these other girls in to a better life, but some are deaf/blind to her newfound life. I was honestly shocked that she's an assistant pastor in her church. She is also happily married now with kids. She was responsive to the awakening and she isn't shy to share her story with younger girls, which is absolutely amazing, but it took a while for her to get there. She yielded to the process, which is hard for most of us.

We all have insecurities and they can be a major barrier to letting our light shine. The goal for all of us should be to become secured in our insecurities, but whilst that is the goal, we should still let our light shine in every way we can. A friend told me that she wasn't comfortable in her skin and she had really bad experiences with it. She would have severe reactions and she never wanted to come out of her house. It was mental torture and she is still getting over it gradually, but she knows who she is now and understands that she is more than acne. She now runs a blog to share her story- how she pulled through the tough times and how she is getting on with the treatments and life. Another friend was really obese and similarly, she wouldn't step out of her house. She was bullied and thought life was pointless, but when she understood who she was and built her confidence naturally with the help of God, she then got into the gym and started eating healthily. She said to me, 'if I had just lost weight and didn't deal with the insecurities first, I would still be very insecure even in my new shape that's exciting the boys.' She has released a book now to share her story and help others. In both scenarios, they were really broken and had to find their identity and understand who they were. That only happened after they yielded to the awakening and started to fight their battles.

Another friend's awakening happened after his wife left him when their child was just 10 months old. She left him because he was constantly cheating and this is a lesson for everyone- it was all fun and games until it hit the celling and she wouldn't have it anymore. She got married to him knowing he was cheating, but hoping he would stop (I know you might be thinking, 'who does that?' However, this is minimal compared to the many other mistakes we all make in the name of settling down and getting married). Anyway, he didn't stop cheating, she left and their marriage didn't last two years. He believed he was a man enjoying life until that happened to him and it broke him. I didn't even understand how broken he was until I went to see him and he had overdosed on drugs- from that one experience, he was now battling with a few other things. This got him to sit up and forced him to run to God. He is now back with his wife and life is good, but it took him over three years to get through the mess and then have her back in his life. That experience was what forced him to God and to becoming a better person. He is currently running a mentoring series on how to become a better man, which he said has been a success and keeps him in check.

We all have stories. We need to share our stories and encourage ourselves and others- we are not alone on this journey. A lot of us get carried away and start to act 'brand new', forgetting where we have come from ourselves. I understand that with the newfound life, you have to be careful and also protect your grounds, as I covered in one of the earlier chapters, which is fair, but remember to also encourage, share with and be there for others. Do not chastise people, welcome them.

I have written this book because everyone thinks that my change was drastic, but if I'm going to be honest, it wasn't. I went through a four year transition that most people did not see. It kicked off in Nigeria but I only became intentional about it when I came back to the UK in 2016 and now it is time to grow properly into my purpose.

Do not believe the stories you see on the 'gram. As entertainment is my background, it really gave me exposure. It is really what it's called – showbiz. It is all show business. You would be surprised that half of these people we see living flashy lives aren't genuinely happy and we are here shouting 'goals', signifying that it is what we want. You see romantic relationships online, and you are shouting 'goals', but you have no idea what the relationships are really like.

Vulnerability creates connections- your brokenness is how you connect with others. Everyone knows the right thing from the wrong thing, but many people feel alone. Our situations are not the same but we all have struggles, so you need to identify with people more and let them know we are all in this together.

## Feeling the pressure yet?

Pressure is something that both the saved and the unsaved have to endure, but the difference is that the saved know that despite the pressure, it is all for God's glory. The pressure is there to build something in you- there is always a reason God makes us go through things.

To whom much is given, much is expected and this applies to everyone. We have all been given some sort of talent or gift. Nobody is empty, but the outcome all depends on us choosing either to fight, or to embody emptiness.

Good for you if you don't need to know God to find purpose, but you need him to fulfil it rightly. One thing I will say to you is, whether you like it or not, your gifts come with pressure and how you handle the pressure all depends on knowing who you are in God!

Thinking about it now, I do not blame the servant who hid his talent in the parable of the talents in the Bible.
The 'Parable of the Talents', in Matthew 25:14-30 tells of a master who was leaving his house to travel, and, before leaving, entrusted his property to his servants. According to

the abilities of each man, one servant received five talents, the second servant received two talents and the third servant received one talent. Upon returning home after a long absence, the master asked his three servants for an account of the talents he entrusted to them. The first and the second servants explained that they each put their talents to work and have doubled the value of the property with which they were entrusted. Each servant was rewarded.

Their master said to them, 'Well done, good and faithful servant. You have been faithful over a little; I will set you over much. Enter into the joy of your master.'

The third servant, however, did it differently:
'Then the one who had received the one talent came and said, "Sir, I knew that you were a hard man, harvesting where you did not sow, and gathering where you did not scatter seed, so I was afraid, and I went and hid your talent in the ground. See, you have what is yours."'

His master punished him:
'But his master answered, "Evil and lazy servant! So you knew that I harvest where I didn't sow and gather where I didn't

scatter? Then you should have deposited my money with the bankers, and on my return, I would have received my money back with interest! Therefore, take the talent from him and give it to the one who has ten. For the one who has will be given more and he will have more than enough. But the one who does not have, even what he has will be taken from him. And throw that worthless slave into the outer darkness, where there will be weeping and gnashing of teeth."'

This parable is scary- to think that if we do not use the gifts God has given us, then we are in for it. Honestly, I can relate to the third servant- He is thinking, I do not want this man's trouble. Let me just keep his talent for him and when he comes, I will return it to him because I know the way he can be. Unfortunately, that is not what God wants. With the little he gives us, we should make something out of it- turn a seed into a tree. I guess the servant thought he knew God, but clearly, he didn't! Except for the trouble from his master, the third guy would also have been thinking, why should I go through all the stress and pressures to then lose out the single talent and get into trouble? When God gave the talent, he also gave the trouble you will go through with it. It would have been good if this parable told us how easy it was for the other two servants to double their gifts. It most certainly wouldn't have been easy, but they really knew their master! They knew that no matter what the outcome was, as long as they were engaging their gifts and using them, he would be pleased with them, and they knew that he would come through for them in their weakest moment- he was a wealthy man anyway!

The process of doubling talents is no joke- to even mange the one talent you have is a lot of work already, especially when it comes with so much adversity. We all use the word 'persevere' a lot, but do we really know what it means to persevere? I am still trying to understand it myself because what I have realised is, there are levels to perseverance. As gifted people, we need to be discerning, and the only way we can discern rightly is by having the Holy Spirit – he is our helper. We live in a world that pressures us to accept what it has to offer- it really offers many things that look good but are empty.

I always had my gifts. I knew I would be influential. The signs were obvious, but the question was whether I would stand the test of time. Your gifts and talents come with so much pressure and the more they are manifested, the bigger the pressure. People will pick up this book and think that coming into church or becoming saved means they can engage and manifest their dreams without pressure. If that is you, unfortunately the pressure is more. In the previous chapter, I wrote about not being perfect. Manifesting your gifts comes with the expectation that you should be perfect, which already means pressure, because people forget that gifted people make mistakes.

There are times when the pressure is not even from a mistake you have made- it could come from an immediate or extended family member. John Terry, the former Chelsea football player, had a parent that shoplifted and it was all over the news. Some might say it is just an embarrassing situation, but that is extra pressure on top of whatever pressure he might be under already. Whether you like it or not, it would be at the back of your mind and would most likely affect productivity or the ability to function well. TD Jakes' daughter Sarah Jakes getting pregnant at 13 was serious pressure on TD Jakes, a man held in really high esteem. Do you understand the pressure he must have been under? A pastor of a 30,000-member church! He was sitting on the boards of various government/community organisations. How many people would survive that? These days, you hear of people committing suicide- it is all to do with the pressure they are under.

For the talented too, do not get carried away when you start manifesting your gifts. Look at celebrities that have come, gone and are still here- it is not easy living their lifestyle. A lot of them give in to drugs like most of us do and it gets even worse when they are caught out. Justin Bieber said that the peace he got when he rededicated his life to Christ was something he couldn't explain. I can relate- I couldn't imagine what he went through, because the little fame I experienced and the pressure that came with it wasn't something I could handle. So as you manifest your talents and gifts, please understand that there will be pressure, but what I understand now is that we also have the Holy Spirit. Real peace comes with that- an unexplainable peace which is part of the benefits of my transition. I am now wired differently. In the past, I was the one putting myself under pressure- unnecessary pressures to save face.

Do you know what is funny about the past? Your past only haunts you when you leave it- it is all fine when you stay in it. The only way you get past your past is by moving to another level. To get to higher ground, you need to understand that it is work, which is where I am now. Ever since I understood the reason I was gifted, I have been under real pressure to succeed for God, just like the guy with the five talents.

## *Extract from 'I am More' by Tolu Fabiyi*

We were renting spaces in each other's hearts and we refused to be evicted.
We tried being friends, but it was hard to adjust, so we kept up with appearances,
When we mistakenly find love in a place that is more than friends yet less than love.
Not quite in a relationship but might as well be…
No matter how we tried to re-write the story we knew how it would end, we knew better…

See, I don't understand,
what's the point of building memories that won't last forever, when you and I know that we will only last temporarily together?
What's the point of giving me your last name, if it's not the last one I'll carry? I'm sorry to burst your bubble but I'm not one to date for dating sake…

I am worthy of Love and Affection,
I am a diamond, a rose, a pearl and the most stunning of God's creation,
I am me, unique and different just as God intended for me to be.   It just took me a while to figure that out…

So I was told, first date movies,
second date dinner,
third date altar
because we have no time for games
because we have to be intentional
So when I tell you that I am not ready, please understand,
Let God finish moulding me.
Trust me by the time HE is done, you would say I was worth the wait.
Because I know I am more than what I am.
Is that too much to ask?

# The question I get asked all the time

Since I'm sharing everything, let's talk about dating and where I am right now. There is no day I am not asked about the imaginary girlfriend everyone thinks I have.

To think that I would look forward to being someone's husband is actually funny. I never thought I would commit myself to someone. God and his sense of humour- forever having banter with our plans. The plan was to just have two kids, one baby mum or maybe two and live my life not committed to anyone. I didn't really care about what would happen to the woman/ women that bore the kids. Now I am actually excited to start a family built on Godly values.

I get asked about my relationship status only God knows how many times in a week. Even when I tell people I'm single, they do not believe me. The people that know I am single still ask 'how far?' meaning, is there any update? They are always looking for updates. While transitioning, I did a lot of self-evaluation. I knew I wasn't ready for a relationship even though a lot of people felt I was- talk about judging a book by its cover. People felt like I had everything required to be someone's husband (not even boyfriend). Well, maybe not everything, but the basics that can be built on. I knew deep inside of me that I wasn't there yet. When I said to people that I wasn't ready, I would hear things like, 'you will never be ready, you learn on the job'. I understood this but I still knew I wasn't there yet. There were other priorities I had to face if I didn't want to be a disaster to someone's life. The joke is that friends would ask me for advice and I would give them what they believed was great advice because they would apply it and it would work for them, but I still knew that I wasn't ready.

I needed to understand what it meant to be in a committed romantic relationship, because I have never been in one. As I had said before, I only had people I was 'seeing', so there was no commitment whatsoever, at least from my side anyway. A few of my friends and I used to call me '*Mr. Love them leave them*'. I just didn't care and was reckless with girls.

So I took time off speaking to anyone, dating anyone or breaking anymore hearts. While I was taking this break, females showed interest and I remember saying to one of them that I was not ready and didn't want to hurt her. I told her how I had enough people that did not like me anymore and had only managed to reconcile with some in recent times. She said, 'well it's not you that would get hurt, it's me.' She later got mad that I still wouldn't give in. The hard part was that she was my type on paper, but I had to be firm at that point. Now, she is happily engaged.

Fast forward to recently, I thought, let's try this dating thing. I was in a much better place and understood what dating meant. I had become a man, at least to an extent. I had also found a side to myself that I didn't know was there all this time- a caring and sweet side. I realised that the more I matured, the more that side came out. My boys were even starting to wonder what had come over me.

My first dating experience post-transition made me realise that it wasn't going to be as easy as I thought, or as easy as it seemed for everyone else to find the one. I met my date through her friend. I didn't realise that her friend was also interested, which literally added another level of complication. Anyway, we both liked each other and thought let's give it a go, but something wasn't right and when I prayed about it, I was having crazy dreams, some of which later manifested. Obviously, when you like someone and emotions get involved it is all a bit 'cray cray'. I had made a pledge to God that I would only date intentionally - with purpose- and anything that was a waste of time should be revealed immediately. However, when the dreams were coming and all the physical madness was happening, I still didn't pay attention because emotions were involved. God was speaking and I wasn't listening. I had another dream and that was the final straw- it was a really scary one and at that point, I had to pray some crazy prayers. When things manifested in the physical, I knew it could have only been God- I didn't want to hurt her and was scared to call it quits abruptly, so I was trying to come up with a strategy. Whilst trying to come up with a strategy, the break came from her side. She spoke recklessly and said things she didn't mean- she even said she was over it. She said it and didn't realise what she had said- she tried to come back a few times after, but that was never going to happen.

As much as boys might not like to admit it, in the same way that girls like attention, boys like it too. I was confused with the attention that I got from all sorts of people- it wasn't unusual, but it had increased to another level - even old flings were crawling back. I was trying to understand what the sauce was. Even boys I knew that were richer, more handsome and driving the latest Germans, would still say things like 'give me one, guy. Do you want them all to yourself?' I was confused because these are guys that I wouldn't mind being like (not literally, but you get my drift). The guys saw the way the females drew to me and thought I was dating all of them.

Someone even once said to me, 'you need to decide and pick one because you are people's prayer point'. The attention had become silly. I remember someone else telling me to just pick one and do the damn thing, as though females were items, forgetting the fact that they were also carried for 9 months in someone's belly. I stopped giving out my number at one point – I was honestly confused by all the attention.

Maybe I put myself under a lot of pressure, but getting married is a lot deeper than just the wedding day. I am not looking for perfect because I am not perfect myself, but we all have deal breakers- I don't think I have too many of those. I wouldn't date just for the fun of it- it is too expensive, time-wasting and draining. I am only dating intentionally - purposefully.
I know the pressure is on for many people. Parents are not helping either. My mum recently bought me a book, 'How to

stop looking for perfect and find someone to love'. That is pressure indirectly and it made me think, do I come across as someone looking for perfect? Someone told me that I have really high standards and she did not think that I gave people a chance. I wasn't sure how I felt about that statement- I think we should all know our worth and have a benchmark of what we want. Am I aiming too high for something I am not worth? Am I scaring potentials away with my behaviour or personality? She said that I'm a high achiever and a lot of girls would feel like they can't match me. That got to me! I am usually open about what I am doing or up to, but subconsciously, because of this statement, I became a little closed. I stopped sharing as I did before. My thinking was, if I do not share, no one will know what I am achieving or have achieved, so I would not scare 'potentials' away.

I tried to date someone after the first experience I shared previously and she turned me down. She wasn't interested, which was a hard pill to swallow. I have never been turned down by a female and it was a really humbling experience. I caught the 'L'- I took the loss. We both couldn't really handle the situation at first and it was going to become really awkward. I was going to ignore her and some of my friends that knew what the situation was even advised me to ignore her and be spiteful- make her feel a type of way- which apparently is what you do in those situations. I honestly couldn't. God was clear – 'if you have been preaching on intentional relationships to people, this is the time you put it to practice, regardless of what happens'. I stood and fought for our friendship, which came with a lot of humility, but I had trained myself that rejection should never breed hatred.

So, lessons I have learnt:

- Attraction is Key. I do not just mean physical attraction. Something must attract you to this person. If you are not attracted to them and you force it, in the end you will have yourself to blame.

- Have deal-breakers /look out for red flags. I am a firm believer in having deal breakers and enforcing them in relationships. I don't do primary or secondary deal breakers like some people do- I only have a set of deal breakers and I have shared it with people and everyone seems to agree that they are fair.

- When a guy knows, a guy knows. He will chase you if he wants you. You just need to be discerning and honest with yourself. Shooting your shot isn't attractive. I used to think, why not shoot your shot? If it works, it works, but what I have realised is that it is easier for boys to accept a 'no' than the other way round. So if you know you can't take the no or collect an 'L', just move on and do not shoot your shot.

- Emotions/Feelings do not make sense. I learned this through my first experience after I decided to start dating. I could have decided to go ahead with that situation, but I would have been deceiving myself because I had the warning signs. I decided to ignore for a while, but I came to my senses, as marriage is for a lifetime.

- Unequal yoking is real. Thank God I haven't fallen victim, but not to be rude, I look at a lot of my friends (females and males) now that have rushed into something with someone they do not share the same values/principles with. The majority aren't together anymore- the ones together are basically doing it to save face. Marriage isn't a show or an event - that is the wedding. We all get excited for the ceremony and forget that there is a lifetime after that day.

- Celebrate love! 'OMG', we as black men need to become more responsible and celebrate our wives. I see a lot of that these days and I am super excited, because the generation behind will emulate this and things can only get better. When I see young/old couples that celebrate each other and I see the genuine love they have in their relationship, I always celebrate them because it is something some of us weren't used to growing up.

# Dear entrepreneurs/creatives

**Dear entrepreneur/creative – is it really working?**

Life got real, so I had to get real myself. My mum wasn't going to lend me any more money- I had to get a job. God is really faithful- I got the first job that I sent an application and was interviewed for – an admin role in Tower Hamlets council. The crazy part was that they had someone more experienced than I was. That person ticked all the boxes, but I got the job because there was something about me the senior manager really liked. The manager was not too keen, but he used to work in construction so we had a discussion around tradesmen (dealing with them and how interesting they are), and this was the reason he was happy to give me the job. He knew the contract manager was trying to get rid of him, so he was scared that he would be replaced with me. His fears were not far-fetched. Carlos the manager couldn't construct a sentence and his handwriting was so illegible that even he couldn't read what he wrote most times. I was already being noticed and was becoming a threat to him- one of the supervisors even said it. He said that he had been told to gang up with another colleague and complain about the quality of my work, because the contract manager liked me and kept talking about how to keep me interested in the job. After that conversation with my supervisor, I noticed a pattern amongst two of my colleagues – of negative energy and a lot of complaining. I hadn't even passed probation which was meant to be three months- I had only been there for just over a month.

The hostility became too much and I had a prayer meeting one evening and it was all I prayed about. The morning when I woke up, I just dumped my CV on one of those jobs' websites. In the afternoon, I got a call that my CV had been picked up. I was asked if I would be interested in a job with one of the big four. At that time, I didn't know what the big four were, so I had to google them. I went back and said yes, that I wouldn't mind, so the recruiter said that he would submit my CV and get back to me. My CV was not great, but God had a plan! Fast-forward a few weeks- the recruiter called me after tests and interviews and said that I got into PwC. It was the same scenario- there were other people more qualified with better experiences, but the Director really liked me. I had spoken about what we were trying to do with The HappyMan- that was what got him and I remember he had said that he would like to be the HappyMan and I had said in response, 'of course why not!'

My PwC journey started and it's been really interesting. I didn't think that I would settle in as quickly as I did. I had never worked in a corporate environment, so coming in to a high intensity workplace that still managed to be relaxed was different. I had to learn so much in such little time- my contract was initially temporary, and by the end of my third week, they already wanted to make it permanent. It was actually a permanent role in the first place but they didn't want to give the job straight away just based on a CV, knowing how intense the work could get. I also had the opportunity to be part of One Young World (OYW) - OYW is global platform that connects the brightest young leaders from around the world, empowering them to make lasting connections to create a positive change. I got to work one day- the daily internal newsfeed popped up and there was something about the OYW annual summit. I made an application and made it through the first round out of so many applications. Whilst waiting for the results from the application to represent PwC at OYW, I met Ben, who would eventually become my senior manager in a new team that had just been set up. If you know me, you know how passionate I am about business, people and politics. I am naturally drawn to anything that has to do with these topics. The Multicultural

Business Network society at PwC had partnered with the Entrepreneurs' Network to deliver an event to talk about being a 9-5er and running a side hustle. I saw the ad and it was interesting, so I signed up for it and Ben was the one championing the Entrepreneur's Network. He was one of the facilitators on the night and he did a brief introduction about himself. I knew I had to connect with him because I didn't know that his role (Business Designer) existed at the firm and I was just curious as to what his daily duties at the firm could be.

I connected with him on the day and we agreed to have a catch-up. We had our first catch-up and it felt like he was just the replica of me. He shared his journey so far, how he also went to Africa to work with some farmers and so on. Then he said we should arrange another catch-up as soon as possible because he had something he thought I might be interested in. At the second catch-up, he dropped the bomb and said there was a new team being set up in the firm and the team's job is to discover another 'google'-like idea. He would be the one leading the team working directly with some partners in the technology and investment practice. He asked what I thought of the idea of the team and whether I would be willing to come on board – I burst into tears! I became so emotional that it was unreal. Coming up with ideas and bringing it to fruition is what I love to do- I have so many ideas but I haven't been that flexible with my resources, so there are a lot of things I can't do. This is an opportunity to be paid to do what I love- I am going to be living my purpose in this firm! I didn't have to think twice- I accepted the offer. By the time you read this book, I would have started in this new team, getting paid to live the purpose I was created for. In all of these, I was praying and believing. At different stages, I would be discouraged, but I kept at it. Even though it was hard, I stayed positive and kept pushing because I had learnt to ignore the crowd. Those are the times you would wish nobody knew you so you could just live your life.

Bashy is a UK rapper, for those that do not know him, and he had a major hit in 2007 called 'Black boys'. He had other songs on the charts and was doing well for himself, but somewhere along the lines, things stopped going well. He had to become a bus driver! Imagine going from my TV screen to driving the bus I am on- I think you need to pause and process that. A lot of people wouldn't be ready to do that- I remember on twitter, people would laugh at him and say all sorts. He was a well-known face amongst young people but he had to do what he had to do. Fast forward to now, Bashy is a successful actor in L.A- he is starring in the hit TV show, '24: Legacy', amongst others. The same people I saw tweets from back then are the same people praising him now.

# Who gon' stop us now?

*'What then shall we say to all these things? If God is for us, who can be [successful] against us?' [Romans 8:31Amp]*


Everything I do now is all for God's glory. He is my senior partner in life- be it at work, in business, relationships- anything I am getting involved in. The HappyMan is my personal project, but my email signature says Managing Partner because God is the Lead Partner. I'm in partnership with God on it- it is his project, I am just managing it, so before any decision is made, I go to him. I tried to do it all by myself before and I know the outcome, so these days I consult the Lead Partner first and things are a whole lot easier, and there is evidence of the progress. Whatever you do, always have it at the back of your mind that it should always be for his glory. He should always be at the centre of everything you do.

The people of Babylon wanted to create something epic, which is great, but their ambition wasn't right. They wanted to build a tower to heaven – quite bold and courageous,. I am climbing Kilimanjaro this year and I am trying to imagine if the Babylonians thought that heaven was at the top of Everest? When I came across this story and read it, it resonated with me in a funny way. God is actually on banter- he is actually funny and has an amazing sense of humour. It was that funny feeling for him to say, 'how dare you think you can do it by yourself now that I have given you the framework? How dare you decide that this is what I am going to do with the brand, little boy?' It was a weird feeling. As I am writing this, I can feel him and I can hear him laughing in my face. 'Little boy I knew you before I formed you'.

He had a reason for giving me the name, The HappyMan in the car that day. Our mantra is 'Delivering Smiles'. To deliver smiles to the world is definitely bigger than me. Never stop seeking the face of God and having him at the centre of everything you do because having him involved means you will go farther and do more than your will power. From the previous chapter, you could tell that as soon as I aligned myself, things began to fall in place.

The HappyMan is bigger than me- It is a lifestyle brand that will showcase positivity and give hope to everyone. It is a movement, a global movement. It is a movement creating an environment for every vision. Every human should have a vision, but for that vision to come to life, you need the right environment – this is what The HappyMan is creating. I have been called the social reformer a lot of the time and we are already doing a lot of social reforming from the platform.

The HappyMan is not just me, The HappyMan is a community! The HappyMan is us! The HappyMan is you. I get weak at times when I think of how big this is and this is a big benefit of me sticking to the process regardless of what I have encountered so far. It is so easy to give up and throw in the towel, but when you have a vision and have started the journey, all you need is God to direct your path. So I encourage us all to never forget that it is not just about knowing your purpose, but more about staying in him if you want to go far. Do not be in a hurry- be content but not complacent and let us light up this world together.

## *Extract from 'The Race' by Tolu Fabiyi*

Lord am I ready?
With the speed of light, I tighten my shoe lace, mark my position and gaze at that finish line;
This race is yours lord, use me to run it as you wish (I murmured).

'Go'.
Boom – I think I heard the shot;
It's take off;
My body lifts itself;
I'm moving;
10 meters into the race.
'Where are you going? Go back!'
I thought voices in my head were trying to hold me back;
So I looked back – it was a false start.

Angry and frustrated at such wasted effort, I felt a calm wind across my face as I marked my position again;
Then the shot went off; and we moved;
We covered 100 meters;
But I was still moving;
Racing with myself.
When I hit the 150 meter mark, I stopped racing;
I had won! I won at the 100 meter finish line.

Then it dawned on me- The false start was the warm-up I needed;
God was with me.
Sometimes you get lost just running against yourself;
Sometimes you get stuck at the distractions on every corner of the road or meter mark you reach;
and fear creeps in;
You almost feel like you are not going to make it.

Take a step back, squint if you must, but see the goal and fix your gaze on the finish line;
Then ask God to run with you;
Trust His process;
Because victory is at the other side of your fear.

# Epilogue

Looking back now, I have no regrets. I am much happier about the future than the past. I know better now- I know what is at stake and how exciting the future is. I'm content but not complacent. I feel more at peace with myself, even with less of everything that I once had. My inner peace is what radiates externally as joy- that peace is something I can't explain in words. It is a feeling that I can't describe – an out of this world feeling. I have said throughout the book that 'life is a set-up', but we have the autonomy to make our decisions and change our story or re-write a legacy. Do not look back in regret- every decision you have made got you this far and it has moulded or shaped you in a way, regardless of whether you are happy about it or not. Some might say the decisions were out of their hands or their parents made the decisions on their behalf. If that is the case, it is still all part of your story. Now that you know better or can make your own decisions, straighten your paths and make the right decisions going forward. There are chances you might have to make some unpopular decisions or maybe even become unpopular because of your decisions, like I did, not because they aren't the right decisions, but because they do not fit with the standards set by mere mortals like you and me.

We were all created for a purpose and part of that purpose is to be a light in this world. You can't carry on adding to the darkness of the world- there is a generation coming behind and if we do not start lighting up the world again, I wonder what will be left for them. I am not saying that you should take on the challenge to light up the whole world, but if God has given you the grace to do that, then why not? Please go ahead. In your little circle, start a change. In your family, start a change. At work, start a change – every industry needs people with light in them. Be a light that everyone will run to- be an example to others. But before you can do this, the change starts with you – do you need to be lit up yourself?

Don't ever think your situation is too messy and there isn't a way out- yours is not new and neither is mine. Regardless of your mileage, there is a way back to correct your steps. The road back might be long and lonely but remember that you are not alone as long as you have allowed God to lead your new path.

Pride and stubbornness are thieves of your joy. It does not matter the number of men/women you have slept with.

Maybe you have aborted or caused someone to have an abortion; were involved in prostitution (you were a sponsor or had sponsors all over the gaff, were pimped out, pimped people out); were into fraud; were a victim of bullying/ cause of bullying. Or maybe yours is an emotional wound. Whatever it is that you have gone through, it is all part of your story. You went through it for a reason. They say that what doesn't kill you can only make you stronger. God knows your name and your story. He knows what you have experienced and he made you experience and survive it. He is not a wicked God.

You can be the beginning of a restored legacy. You can turn things around and have a new beginning, not just for yourself but for the future generation. Think about your kids- think about the life you want for them. Let's be forward-looking in our thoughts and actions so that we leave this world a better place. You are all you need to become the best version of yourself. To achieve that, there is a commitment- self-sacrifice, dying to your flesh and letting God take the wheel. The majority of us want to become great people. I barely know anyone that doesn't want to be great, be it greatness defined by man or God. The greatness I want is kingdom-driven because that is what matters, not world-driven greatness. If you are like me, make sure you have the right foundation so that when the wind, blows you are still standing firm. A wind could come in form of anything - like rejection. When rejection comes, how will you respond to it? Are you going to stand up, face it and push (because greater is he that lives in you than he who is in the world), or will you run back into hiding (which can also generate anger/bitterness as you wonder why you're facing the difficulty)?

Social Media. I know I spoke about it in the book but I won't close this book without touching again on this blessing that is also eating up a lot of our happiness. It is so much of a blessing that it's now becoming a curse, for lack of a better word. We have heard it again and again that you should not believe the virtual lifestyle people show you online. Most of us would only post a picture because we think it will bang and get the likes. In fact, when we see someone post a picture that is not their best, we question why they have posted such a picture – because they are expected to only show their best self online. The only place where broken marriages look perfect is online. The only place you find people that are naturally not brave seeming brave is online. The online world is a bubble and you have to keep constantly reminding yourself that these lifestyles people portray is virtual and not their reality. I am sure we all know someone that has a beautiful virtual life but a dark reality. Also, because you are the light of the world or will soon take up that mantel, do not join in painting a perfect lifestyle online because someone is also out there looking at your pages – this person needs to see the reality. Practise what you preach- be the light or social media!

Do not beat yourself down or ever disqualify yourself. The fact that you still wake up daily means that God is not done with you regardless of the bad decisions you have made or the issues of life. Be open, and like me, maybe try it out for six months intentionally and let God direct your steps. You might not be the best at what you do but remember that you are different. Come out of the bubble, SIT DOWN and get ready to fight, excel and SIT UP.

I hope you have been inspired and recognise that it is time to re-write your story. Whether it seems you are on top of your game or not, always ask yourself – is God involved?

# Transformation – Princess Ashilokun

*Transformation*
*(noun)*
*1. a marked change in form, nature, or appearance.*
*2. a metamorphosis during the life cycle of a plant.*

*(Seed)*

*Speak life into your own story,*
*Watch it unravel from your tongue,*
*find out how*
*a tale is always*
*harder to tell when you are telling the chapter*
*you are still going through.*

*(Root)*

*Reflect on how the voice of fear*
*buzzing boldly between your ears*
*made you forget*
*how to silence its sound,*
*how to grow faster*
*than the shadows*
*of your insecurities.*

*(Stem)*

*Navigating darkness comes easy,*
*dark thoughts find shade*
*in a mind that has stopped*
*letting the light in from Him.*
*Bend your life's will and soon find*
*you form a chrysalis*
*of His making.*

*(Flower)*

*It takes an ocean and time
to change the coastline. Neither ocean floor
nor the shapes of the shore
are formed by a single tide.*

*(Fruit)*

*Pause,
Take a breath, exhale.
Recognise that transformations
occur easiest when
the person you are realises
that the vision of the person
you still wish to be
is waiting
on the other side
of the hard work
you still refuse to put in.*

# Acknowledgements

With every vision/goal, you need the right resources to make it happen! A lot of times, you do not know how these things will come together, but with God, everything will always work together for your good. Putting this piece together has been a journey and a very different experience for me! Apart from God who we know is first, this book would not have happened during this last year had it not been for some amazing people. There is a long list of people and I can't mention every single person, so I have categorised everyone.

My family! These people were there in my darkest and brightest times. You kept my feet on the ground, even when I couldn't help but keep 'jumping'. I couldn't imagine the world without you – thank you Dad, Mum, Tomi and Toni.

I give enormous heartfelt thanks to my friends and extended family. You have put up with this annoying boy for the longest. Not a lot of people can stand me, but you have been there and I pray I will always be available when you need me. This book's project team. Everyone that helped from inception in any capacity (advising, writing, editing, reading, publishing, planning the launch) with this piece of art! Thank you- you are the real MVPs!

The lovely poets that willingly gave me their pieces to insert in this book. I look forward to seeing you at the top! Your work will take you to places you never imagined.

My TLC family! I am grateful to you for accepting me the way I was! I honestly believe that God had me in mind when he gave TLC's leadership its mandate.

My work family! Thank you for accepting me, even with my zero knowledge of the corporate world!

To everyone out there trying to change their story and live an example whilst empowering others to make the world a better place. Keep at it- do not stop and it will be all smiles and light in the end!

Merci.